Invisible Upgrades

Invisible Upgrades

How Technology Changes Us Without Asking

Rowan Hale

Mindful Pages

Published in 2025

ISBN: 9789371773218 (PB)
ISBN: 9789371773294 (eBook)

Published by

Mindful Pages
Imprint of Alpha Editions LLC
312 W. 2nd St #1834
Casper, WY 82601, USA

This book was developed using advanced writing tools to support the drafting and ideation process. All content has been thoughtfully curated, refined, and reviewed to ensure quality and relevance.

Content

Introduction
The Unnoticed Trade

We seldom recognise the precise moment when a new technology slips into our lives. A software update installs itself overnight. A device arrives, gifted or upgraded, without much ceremony. A feature appears—pre-enabled—and we rarely bother to switch it off. There is no sense of crossing a threshold, no deliberate weighing of what we gain against what we might lose. Instead, the shift is gentler, almost imperceptible: a slow, ambient drift. Familiar routines begin to tilt. The tools that once served us start to shape our thoughts, our values, and even the things we quietly forget how to do on our own.

This book is about that drift—the subtle, almost invisible upgrades that promise frictionlessness while quietly redrawing the inner map of our attention, memory, choices, and skills. We never voted to outsource our navigation to GPS, our spelling to autocorrect, or our social validation to notifications. These transformations were not publicly debated. They arrived piecemeal, often dressed in the language of convenience, speed, and personalisation. Yet taken together, they have produced a deep behavioural rewiring—one that has redefined what it means to know, to choose, to act with competence, and, perhaps most importantly, to remain human in an age of constant mediation.

Technology doesn't seek our permission to change us. It simply alters the environment around us—and we, as ever, adapt.

Discussions of digital technology tend to fall into two camps: anxious alarm or uncritical enthusiasm. What's often missing is a chart of the middle terrain, that grey space where most of us actually live. This book does not stand to condemn technology, nor to absolve it. Instead, it seeks to map the small, unremarked exchanges that accumulate quietly over time: the momentary discomfort we trade for convenience; the spontaneous choice rerouted by an algorithmic nudge; the dormant skill, neglected because a device now performs it more efficiently.

These aren't dramatic stories. They are incremental ones. They take shape across hundreds of micro-moments each day—shaping us through what we no longer have to think about, recall, or question. The bargains we make are rarely announced. But that doesn't make them trivial.

Take navigation. In exchange for the astonishing ability to know the best route anywhere within seconds, we've forfeited the skill of orienting ourselves without assistance—the ability to hold mental maps, to dwell in uncertainty long enough to discover something by accident. Or consider information: we now have immediate access to near-limitless knowledge, yet retain remarkably little of it. Our minds defer to databases that never sleep, and in doing so, sidestep the slower, more effortful work of understanding and memory. Increasingly, our days are governed by default settings—curated feeds, pre-selected options, algorithmically "personalised" choices that gently steer our attention.

These are the trades we never consciously agreed to, the decisions we never quite made.

The question is not whether technology is useful—it plainly is—but what happens when use becomes unexamined. Each chapter of *Invisible Upgrades* explores a specific domain where small shifts in design and habit have produced disproportionate changes in cognition, autonomy, and culture. From how we navigate our cities to how we remember phone numbers, from the decisions we delegate to algorithms to the identities shaped by our data, this book investigates the hidden architecture underlying our daily digital existence.

Consider, for instance, the interface of a shopping app. At first glance, it offers abundance: infinite scrolling, endless choice. Yet beneath that surface lies a quiet choreography. Filters apply themselves. Ratings appear pre-sorted. Products are ranked not by objective relevance but by probability—what you are statistically most likely to click, not necessarily what best suits you. What looks like freedom is, more often, a gently narrowing corridor. What feels efficient can be a subtle form of behavioural constraint.

Not sinister, perhaps—but hardly neutral.

Design has become a quiet form of governance, shaping not only what we do, but what we expect to do, what we notice, and what never occurs to us to question. Every new device comes pre-configured; the opt-in is, by design, automatic. To resist or reconfigure demands time, expertise, and energy—three commodities already in short supply in overstimulated lives.

Gradually, we take the easier path. We stop sketching directions by hand. We forget the things we once remembered without effort. We allow algorithms to lead the dance. Skills that lie unused begin to atrophy. The danger isn't that technology alone erodes our abilities—it's that it does so quietly, while we interpret the process as progress. Ease masquerades as improvement; speed, as evolution. But perhaps these comforts conceal a quieter kind of loss.

This book argues that not all friction is waste, not all slowness inefficiency, and not all delegation liberation. Sometimes, the struggle itself was what built competence, patience, or care. When technology removes difficulty, it doesn't necessarily remove cost—it merely delays or displaces it.

Remembering a birthday, for instance, is not just an act of recall but of affection—a small gesture of attention that says, *I remembered you.* When a calendar app automates the reminder, the function is fulfilled, but the emotional texture thins. The ritual becomes mechanical. Similarly, predictive text smooths communication but can flatten expression. Language starts to feel prefabricated, its edges sanded off.

The central question of *Invisible Upgrades* is not whether technology is good or bad, but who we are becoming as we stop doing certain things ourselves.

Every tool carries an old truth: what we create, in turn, creates us. The pencil externalised our thoughts. The clock synchronised our sense of time. The camera reshaped our memory and our presence in the world. Today's technologies differ only in speed and subtlety. They blend into daily life so seamlessly that their influence becomes invisible—and therefore harder to interrogate.

To see them clearly, we must first pause. We must name the exchanges we're making, notice the features we never chose, and examine the defaults we've silently accepted. The right question is no longer just *what does this tool do for me?* but *what is it doing to me?* And—perhaps more urgently—do those effects align with the kind of life I wish to live?

This book does not preach digital abstinence, nor pine for a pre-digital past. It invites something harder and more mature: discernment. The capacity to notice the quiet transformations, to understand their cumulative power, and to reclaim, where meaningful, the manual mode—not as nostalgia, but as an act of agency.

Technology will continue to evolve, as it should. Yet as it becomes more ambient, predictive, and entangled with our sense of self, we face a growing responsibility: to develop inner tools strong enough to coexist with the outer ones consciously, not passively.

The chapters ahead explore this subtle frontier—where tools become habits, and habits harden into identity. Where ease turns to expectation, and expectation into dependence. But also where, with a touch of awareness and deliberate effort, we can recover what we didn't mean to relinquish.

This is not a manifesto against technology. It is an invitation to notice—and, in that noticing, to reclaim the simple, radical freedom to choose.

Chapter 1
The Convenience Contract

We live amid a quiet chorus of consent. Few of us can recall the moment we agreed to the countless terms and permissions that now underpin our digital existence. The "I agree" button, once a rare formality, has become a reflex—a gesture so habitual it barely registers. And yet, hidden within those effortless taps lies a system of contracts that extend far beyond legality. They shape how we behave, how we think, and, over time, who we imagine ourselves to be. What we've accepted isn't simply convenience—it's compliance.

Convenience has become such an embedded value in modern life that we scarcely notice its rule. We call it efficiency, innovation, user-friendliness. But it is more than a perk—it is an ideology, a design language that rewrites the relationship between humans and systems. We speak of choice, customisation, optimisation. Yet often, these choices exist within invisible frames, bounded by options pre-selected by designers and algorithms. "Smart" tools and seamless interfaces don't merely remove friction; they redirect behaviour, ushering us down predetermined paths. And, for the most part, we oblige.

This chapter examines what might be called the *convenience contract*—a pact entered into without signatures or ceremony. It requires no deliberation, no announcement. It thrives on ease and enforces itself through what designers term *preference architecture*: interfaces structured to make certain decisions feel effortless and others burdensome. The result is not coercion but quiet choreography, where our freedom of choice remains technically intact but practically diminished.

Agency, in this arrangement, begins to migrate—from the user to the system.

Consider the ritual of setting up a new smartphone. Within minutes, we've agreed to location tracking, permitted dozens of apps to collect data, and tethered our accounts across multiple platforms. It feels seamless, almost personal. But the structure is anything but neutral. Each step is engineered for compliance. The effort required to alter defaults—to resist—demands patience and skill few possess, or care to acquire. The asymmetry is intentional. It is, quite literally, built in.

This quiet surrender is what behavioural economists describe as *passive drift*. It stems from *default bias*, the tendency to accept pre-selected options because deviation requires effort. The phenomenon is well documented: countries with opt-out organ donation systems exhibit dramatically higher participation rates than those requiring explicit consent. The difference isn't moral—it's mechanical. People stick with defaults. Technology, ever observant, has perfected this principle. Its systems presume acceptance, and overwhelmingly, they receive it.

What makes today's convenience contract so powerful is the sophistication of design that enforces it. Modern user experience (UX) is lauded for its invisibility—the smoother, the better. But invisibility should never be mistaken for neutrality. Every design decision—what's highlighted, what's hidden, what comes pre-enabled—reflects a set of assumptions about human behaviour. Infinite scroll, autoplay, the colour of the confirmation button—none of these are arbitrary. They are subtle nudges, habit-shapers in visual form.

Dark patterns make this explicit. A subscription that renews easily but cancels painfully. A cookie prompt that offers one bright "accept all" button beside a labyrinthine "manage preferences" link. These are not glitches—they are strategies.

They play on fatigue, distraction, and our instinct to conserve effort. Legally permissible, ethically questionable, they do not force compliance; they simply make non-compliance harder.

At what point, then, does design stop serving and start steering? The answer emerges in what begins to feel *normal.* Design not only structures experience; it naturalises it. It defines what counts as intuitive, what feels clunky, what we tolerate as "just the way things work." When enough systems are built around the same priorities—speed, smoothness, simplicity—our expectations evolve. We start to crave frictionless processes and recoil from anything that feels slow. Ease becomes synonymous with good design, and, by extension, with good living.

The illusion of choice thrives within this normalisation. We think of the algorithmic menu—recommendations on a streaming platform, product listings in an online shop—as a democratic field of possibility. But these options are pre-filtered, ranked by probabilities that serve the platform's goals. The algorithm doesn't show you the "best"; it shows you the most *engaging*. Popular, familiar, confirmatory. In effect, it learns to mirror you. The more you watch or buy, the narrower the reflection becomes. Abundance becomes repetition.

E-commerce follows the same script. "Relevance" and "personalisation" promise efficiency but conceal commercial incentives: paid placements, behavioural predictions, profitability scores. Behind every effortless choice is an architecture of persuasion. Over time, this normalises passivity. We stop searching for alternatives because we no longer imagine they exist.

Convenience, then, is never neutral. It is structured, motivated, and deeply entangled with power. Every simplification encodes an intention—to keep you scrolling, subscribing, clicking. The elimination of friction is not purely user-centred;

it's profit-centred. A seamless experience discourages scrutiny. People rarely question what feels easy.

We are told technology empowers us, yet much of that empowerment is procedural rather than substantive. We can personalise our feeds, adjust our settings, fine-tune notifications—but always within the sandbox defined by others. Real empowerment lies in the capacity to interrogate the frame itself: to ask why those options exist, who benefits from them, and what happens when we accept their logic unquestioningly.

This is not to say that convenience is inherently malign. Few would argue against the advantages of instant payments or simplified travel bookings. But when convenience becomes the *criterion* by which all systems are judged, we flatten the richness of human experience. We begin to measure success not by depth of understanding, but by lack of effort. Efficiency replaces engagement as the highest good.

Worse, this ethic of ease seeps beyond our screens. It reshapes how we relate—to institutions, to one another, even to ourselves. We grow intolerant of ambiguity, allergic to waiting. We demand frictionless service in domains where friction is essential: learning, relationships, governance. The problem is not technology's efficiency, but our assumption that efficiency is always desirable. Some aspects of life—trust, deliberation, wisdom—cannot be streamlined without losing their meaning.

At heart, the convenience contract is about power and consent. Who sets the defaults? Who profits from our compliance? And who, exactly, is doing the choosing? These are ethical, not technical, questions. To ignore them is to surrender the terms of agency. To confront them is to begin recovering it.

The pages that follow trace how convenience evolved from design principle to ideology—how frictionlessness became both a business model and a worldview. We will examine how small interface choices accumulate into behavioural norms, and how passive drift slowly erodes deliberation in the name of ease. The challenge is not to reject convenience wholesale, but to see it clearly—to ask which forms of ease enrich us, and which quietly impoverish us.

Wanting life to be easier is no sin. But ease is never free. Someone pays for it—in data, in attention, in diminished autonomy. The question, as always, is whether we are paying knowingly, or whether the cost is quietly deducted from our agency, one seamless tap at a time.

Terms We Didn't Read

No one reads the terms. Not really. The vast legal scrolls attached to every app download, software installation, or website visit are skimmed, if at all, and hastily accepted. But the deeper truth is that *we ignore far more than just the legal text.* What we overlook is not merely contractual language, but a far-reaching system of consent woven into the very architecture of the digital world—through default settings, interface design, and pre-optimised options that quietly shape our decisions long before we're even aware we're making them.

The digital environment, at its core, is structured around the concept of default. Defaults are not passive placeholders. They are active behavioural levers, and they work precisely because most people do not change them. This is not a flaw of human nature—it's a function of it. The average user is cognitively frugal, time-constrained, and motivated by simplicity. When faced with a system that offers a seamless "next" button versus a convoluted series of toggles and dropdowns, almost all of us will choose the path of least resistance. And so we accept—not just the settings, but the behavioural assumptions coded into them.

This tendency is not new. Behavioural scientists have long studied the power of defaults, particularly in the context of public policy. In a famous example from behavioural economics, countries with default opt-in organ donation policies consistently report dramatically higher donor rates than those requiring opt-in. The difference is not cultural altruism—it's inertia. The same principle now governs our digital lives, but on a far more intimate scale. We don't actively *choose* to share our location with weather apps, or let platforms track our online behaviour, or have our purchases silently used to build psychographic profiles. We simply don't disable the boxes. And so they remain enabled.

Passive drift into convenience is not a flaw in our attention; it is a feature of systems designed to exploit attentional limits. Each new device or application offers a sense of personalisation and control, but that promise is carefully orchestrated. The onboarding process is efficient, frictionless, and subtly directive. Most users glide through screens asking for access, enabling features, linking data across services. Rarely is it obvious what is optional and what is critical. By the time we reach the home screen, we've agreed to far more than we realise. The settings have become the contract.

What makes this contract so difficult to interrogate is its invisibility. Unlike traditional agreements, which require signatures or discussion, the modern convenience contract is enacted through interface design. It is embedded in the logic of what we're allowed to change, and how hard it is to change it. In a study by researchers at Carnegie Mellon, they found that reading the privacy policies of the 75 most popular websites would take the average user 76 workdays per year. No one is doing that—not because they don't care, but because the architecture of choice is too dense, too opaque, and too optimised for speed over reflection.

Design plays a central role in this landscape—not merely as an aesthetic function, but as a governing force. The field of user experience (UX) design has matured into a sophisticated discipline that blends psychology, data science, and interface engineering. At its best, it enables intuitive interaction. At its worst, it obscures trade-offs under the guise of convenience. Consider the difference between "dark patterns" and persuasive design. The former refers to techniques that trick users—such as hiding unsubscribe buttons or making it harder to cancel than to sign up. The latter is subtler, operating through default flows that gently push behaviour in a desired direction. Both rely on the same premise: the user will not fight the flow unless they have a compelling reason. And compelling reasons are rarely visible.

There is a fundamental asymmetry here between user and designer. The user engages with the interface at surface level. The designer orchestrates what is seen, what is emphasised, and what remains buried. When a social media app pre-selects "on" for data sharing with third parties, that is not a neutral decision. It is a behaviourally engineered assumption. When an e-commerce site defaults to "subscribe and save," or presents bundled pricing designed to steer purchasing, those too are structured choices—ones that reframe what feels normal.

Normality, once established through design, rarely invites scrutiny. After enough exposure, we forget there was ever an alternative. Autoplay becomes expected. Instant feedback becomes necessary. The invisible becomes habitual. And once a behaviour becomes habitual, it ceases to feel like a decision at all. It simply *is*.

This is where the concept of the convenience contract becomes morally and politically significant. Because the decisions embedded in defaults are not just about usability—they reflect priorities, values, and power structures. Who decides what is enabled by default? Who benefits from prechecked boxes? In many cases, the answer is simple: the platform, not the user. Convenience, in this sense, is a persuasive framing. It suggests user empowerment while actually streamlining behavioural conformity.

This conformity, while not inherently malicious, raises complex ethical concerns. Consider smart home devices, which often arrive with microphones activated, data-sharing enabled, and updates pushed remotely without explicit consent. Or consider wearable health trackers that collect intimate biometric data, store it in proprietary clouds, and use it to train predictive algorithms—again, with only cursory disclosures. These are not fringe examples; they are standard practice.

The implications stretch beyond privacy. They shape cognition. When our tools remember things for us—birthdays, passwords, navigation routes—we outsource not just function, but discipline. Over time, we weaken the cognitive muscles once used to retain, recall, or reflect. And because these tools are seamless and pre-optimised, we rarely notice the trade. It feels like an upgrade. Until one day, the skill is gone.

This passive drift—gradual, unexamined, frictionless—is perhaps the defining characteristic of the digital age. It is not that people make bad choices; it's that they're not made aware they are making choices at all. The behavioural economist Cass Sunstein describes this as "choice architecture"—the structuring of decision environments to nudge preferred outcomes. In public health, this can save lives. In digital ecosystems governed by profit motives, it can subtly entrench habits that serve corporate interests while appearing to serve users.

But what makes this especially difficult to counter is the psychological appeal of ease. Friction is cognitively and emotionally taxing. When a system removes barriers, we interpret it as progress. Yet friction often plays a valuable role: it introduces pause, prompts consideration, and allows for the possibility of dissent. A world without friction is one in which resistance is systematically disabled.

This is not an argument for technological regression or luddite nostalgia. Many default-driven systems have enhanced safety, access, and efficiency at scale. The question is not whether we should have pre-set options, but whether we should *be aware* of what they imply. It is the difference between informed consent and behavioural automation. Between using technology and being used by it.

In practical terms, reclaiming awareness begins with cultivating friction where it has been smoothed away too completely. Changing the settings. Reading the disclosures. Questioning the defaults. Even small acts of resistance—choosing not to save passwords, disabling location tracking, adjusting notification thresholds—can act as micro-reminders that the system is not neutral. These are not symbolic gestures; they are assertions of agency.

Yet the responsibility cannot fall solely on the individual. The deeper challenge is structural. It requires a cultural and regulatory reckoning with the ethics of design. Transparency in settings is not enough if users are cognitively overwhelmed. Consent is meaningless if the alternative is buried under six layers of interface logic. What's needed is not just technical literacy, but *consent literacy*: the ability to recognise where our agency has been quietly pre-signed away.

Terms we didn't read are not just a legal oversight. They are a metaphor for the broader condition of the digitally conditioned self: accepting what's given, adapting without awareness, drifting in systems that appear to serve but often shape. To read the terms—truly read them—is to pause, to examine, and, perhaps most importantly, to decide with intention. In a world increasingly designed to think for us, that act of decision may be the most human one left.

When Design Decides

Most people do not realise that every digital choice they make—what they click, ignore, purchase, or dismiss—unfolds within a stage set by someone else. The app does not simply show content. It presents *structured experiences*. The website does not just offer information. It offers *guided interactions*. Design, especially in the realm of user experience (UX), has long since evolved beyond aesthetics or usability. It is now a soft form of governance—quietly prescribing not only how we behave within a system but also what we come to perceive as intuitive, efficient, even moral.

What makes this influence powerful is its invisibility. When a design element feels "natural," we tend not to question it. The scroll is infinite? Of course. The home button disappears after a few seconds? That must be modern minimalism. The default email sorting pushes promotional content out of sight? Convenient. Rarely do we stop to ask: *Whose intentions are embedded in this design? Whose values are being normalised?* Because interface decisions are presented under the guise of smooth functionality, users typically accept them as neutral scaffolding—when in reality, they are laden with assumptions.

This is not a critique of design as manipulation per se. Human environments have always been designed—from roads to classrooms, from libraries to supermarkets. What sets digital design apart is the pace, scale, and behavioural precision it allows. A grocery store might influence your path with shelf placement and lighting. A social media app can redesign your attention span. Both shape behaviour. But only one collects granular feedback in real time, feeding into algorithms that can refine and recalibrate user engagement loops hour by hour.

Design doesn't just respond to what users want—it teaches them what to want. Consider the concept of "infinite scroll," pioneered by Aza Raskin and later adopted widely by social platforms. It eliminated the need to click for more content, producing a frictionless feed of entertainment or information. The result: dramatically increased user engagement, longer sessions, and a new mental model of how content should behave. In Raskin's own retrospective critique, he described it as "behavioural cocaine," an elegant feature that rewrote user expectations while anchoring platforms to addictive time-based metrics.

The success of such design elements lies in their ability to feel like *good design*. They reduce cognitive load, decrease effort, and create a sense of flow. But what is often obscured is that this "flow" serves platform goals as much as user needs. What you see first, how it is arranged, how much effort it takes to exit or question the flow—these are all design decisions, optimised not for reflection or autonomy, but for retention, conversion, and loyalty.

This is the quiet threshold where design transitions from user support to behavioural scripting. Think of Amazon's one-click checkout. It is a masterpiece of convenience, but also of bypass. It sidesteps hesitation, eliminates reflection, and turns shopping into an impulse-confirmation reflex. The user *feels* empowered—they did nothing more than make a swift choice. But the infrastructure beneath is optimised to pre-empt resistance, to eliminate the delay that used to accompany financial decisions. When systems are built to suppress deliberation, what kind of decision-making is left?

Design also sets the contours of what seems normal. When biometric logins become standard, entering a password starts to feel antiquated. When predictive text populates our messages, composing a sentence manually feels unnecessarily laborious. And when every platform offers algorithmically personalised content, unfiltered information begins to seem chaotic or inefficient. Each of these examples reveals a subtle shift—not just in tools, but in baseline expectations. *Design teaches users what to expect, and by extension, what to accept.*

Nowhere is this more apparent than in onboarding flows—the initial moments when users set up a service or install a device. These are designed to be quick, low-friction, and above all, decisive. They offer seemingly personal choices: turn location sharing on or off, enable voice recognition, allow data syncing. But the architecture of these flows is almost always weighted toward compliance. The accept button is bright and large; the reject path, small or buried. Time-pressed users, conditioned by thousands of previous interfaces, follow the most visually or cognitively appealing path. Once again, the design *decides* what most people will choose—without ever removing the illusion of choice.

The illusion is crucial. A truly coercive interface would provoke resistance. But a *persuasive* interface works precisely because it respects just enough of the user's autonomy to feel legitimate. The term "choice architecture," coined by Richard Thaler and Cass Sunstein, captures this duality. It recognises that while users *can* choose differently, the environment in which they choose matters enormously. In a cafeteria, the order of food presentation influences what people eat. Online, the sequence of options, the prominence of buttons, the language of prompts—all shape what people *think* they're freely selecting.

Design also encodes values. Consider how social platforms frame interactions. The heart icon suggests affection or approval, even if the action is a mere acknowledgement. The retweet function amplifies without requiring context. The streak count in apps like Snapchat gamifies communication, shifting social engagement from meaningful exchange to performance metrics. None of these features are inevitable—they are intentional. They construct a behavioural world in which attention is tracked, measured, and publicly validated.

Over time, these design norms don't just shape what users do; they reshape what feels socially acceptable or even necessary.

This is particularly evident in the gamification of everyday tasks. Fitness trackers convert steps into rewards, meditation apps assign streaks, language platforms turn learning into point accumulation. On the surface, these features enhance motivation. But they also risk converting intrinsic activities—walking, learning, reflecting—into instrumentally driven ones. The moment a behaviour is tied to a badge or metric, it becomes susceptible to metric distortion. We start walking for the steps, not for the clarity. Learning for the streak, not the understanding. Design, again, has decided not only how we behave, but *why*.

Of course, defenders of such systems point to their effectiveness. And they are not wrong. Good design makes things easier. It can reduce user errors, enhance accessibility, and foster adoption. But the ethical tension arises when that same ease becomes a vehicle for behavioural steering. The fact that it works does not mean it is neutral. Nor does user satisfaction necessarily reflect informed consent. What we find "satisfying" is often what we've been taught to expect—by the very systems that taught us.

To understand the full power of design, one must look beyond interface elements and into design *philosophy*. A product designed around user delight may prioritise novelty. One designed around user retention may favour habituation. One focused on monetisation will almost certainly prioritise conversion paths. Each philosophy leads to different outcomes, often invisible to the user but deeply influential over time. The problem is not that these priorities exist—it's that they are rarely transparent, and almost never up for public deliberation.

This absence of deliberation becomes especially problematic in systems that scale. A UX choice that affects ten users may be trivial. One that affects a billion can influence cultural norms. The shift from chronological to algorithmic news feeds altered the way people perceive time, relevance, and truth. The design decision was ostensibly about surfacing what matters most. But the criteria were opaque, the incentives misaligned, and the downstream consequences—such as polarisation, filter bubbles, and algorithmic bias—significant. Here, design didn't just decide what users saw. It reshaped what they believed.

The challenge ahead is not to make design less powerful, but to make its power visible—and open to scrutiny. As long as users operate under the impression that design merely serves, they will remain unaware of how often it also steers. And while designers may not intend to manipulate, *intention is not the only metric that matters*. Outcomes do. So too does the capacity of users to interrogate, resist, or reconfigure the systems they inhabit.

For this to happen, a shift in digital literacy is required—not just learning how to use tools, but how to *read* them. To ask: Why is this feature here? Who benefits if I click this? What assumptions are baked into this layout, this prompt, this flow? These questions move us beyond usability into ethical awareness. They restore a measure of deliberation to a landscape built on default acceptance.

When design decides, it shapes not only what is easy but what is *conceivable*. It frames the menu of actions, but also the expectations of what an interface, a platform, or a user should be. In the age of digital immersion, recognising this influence is no longer optional. It is foundational to regaining agency—not by rejecting design, but by refusing to be blindly designed.

The Illusion of Choice

Modern technology often presents itself as a marketplace of limitless options. Scroll through a streaming service, and you'll be offered hundreds—if not thousands—of titles. Open a food delivery app, and you're flooded with cuisines from every corner of the globe. Visit an online retailer, and you're met with what appears to be unbounded freedom: categories, filters, recommendations, and user reviews all seemingly designed to empower the consumer. The surface narrative is abundance. But the structure beneath tells a different story—one of constraint, prediction, and preselection.

Despite the apparent diversity of options, most digital environments are curated to produce specific outcomes. The user believes they are navigating a sea of choices, but the interface quietly narrows those choices in real time—guided by algorithms optimised for engagement, conversion, or retention. You are not wandering freely. You are being ushered.

Take the example of Amazon. A product search yields thousands of results, but the first page captures the overwhelming majority of clicks. Within that first page, "sponsored" listings are often indistinguishable from organic results, except for a faint label. These promoted options aren't necessarily the best, cheapest, or most relevant; they are the most monetisable. The illusion is that users are choosing from a wide field. In truth, most are responding predictably to structured visibility. The architecture of the platform heavily favours outcomes that serve the host company's business goals—nudging you toward products that are most likely to generate revenue, not necessarily satisfaction.

This dynamic is not limited to commerce. On streaming platforms like Netflix or Spotify, personalisation engines present "Top Picks" or "Recommended For You" carousels based on prior consumption. These interfaces suggest a highly individualised experience. Yet studies have shown that these recommendation systems often rely less on your unique preferences and more on predictive clustering—placing users into behavioural categories and serving content that performs well with similar profiles. The result is convergence. Over time, users begin to consume increasingly similar content, narrowing the range of cultural exposure even as the interface claims to diversify it.

Choice, in these contexts, is real in the technical sense—but heavily conditioned in practice. Algorithms do not merely reflect your past behaviour; they *scaffold* your future ones. The more you engage with a platform, the more it learns what you are likely to choose next—and begins shaping your environment accordingly. This is not inherently malevolent. Predictive modelling allows services to be more responsive and reduce cognitive load. But it also introduces a subtle determinism: the path of least resistance is always the path you've taken before.

There is a psychological dimension to this too. Cognitive science tells us that humans are generally poor at distinguishing between self-directed decisions and externally influenced ones—particularly when influence is exerted subtly. When an interface presents three product tiers, with one highlighted as "most popular," many users gravitate to that middle option, assuming it's the rational compromise. Known as the decoy effect, this behavioural nudge exploits our tendency to anchor around what feels typical or socially endorsed. The platform appears neutral. The user feels empowered. But the outcome was largely anticipated.

Even design aesthetics can reinforce the illusion of autonomy. Consider the role of micro-interactions—the animations, transitions, and feedback loops that make digital interfaces feel alive. These elements are not merely decorative. They guide attention, reward engagement, and draw users into loops of behaviour. A flashing notification icon is not a passive alert; it is a behavioural trigger. A swipe-right interaction is not just a convenience; it conditions a mode of decision-making that emphasises speed over deliberation. These design choices cultivate habitual responses—what designers call "stickiness." The more seamless the interaction, the less aware we become of how guided we are.

The issue is not that technology offers too few choices, but that it *presents choices while pre-determining the probable selection*. This distinction is critical. It allows platforms to maintain the appearance of freedom while simultaneously steering behaviour. A user may technically be free to opt out, unsubscribe, or dig into privacy settings—but doing so often requires disproportionate effort, multiple steps, or hidden pathways. This is behavioural friction, strategically placed to discourage deviation from the norm.

Airline booking websites frequently use this tactic. During checkout, users are prompted to add extras—seat selection, baggage, insurance—with pre-selected options or alarming language: "Are you sure you want to continue without travel protection?" These prompts exploit loss aversion, a well-known psychological bias that makes people more sensitive to potential losses than equivalent gains. The user still *chooses*, but the context is engineered to make one option feel safer or more responsible. The company profits from add-ons the customer may not have sought out independently.

What's more, the data trails generated by these interactions feed into machine learning systems that refine the illusion over time. A user who regularly shops for eco-friendly products may begin seeing more "green" options prominently displayed—not because they were the best, but because they align with a profile the platform finds profitable. A person researching medical conditions may be targeted with health product ads that exploit anxiety rather than offering credible information. In each case, the range of visible options is shaped by opaque calculations, not objective merit.

This is where the philosophical stakes emerge. Choice is foundational to modern conceptions of freedom and agency. If the ability to choose is undermined—not through prohibition, but through manipulation—we enter a space where autonomy becomes performative. We *feel* like we're acting freely, while mostly responding to cues embedded in systems optimised to predict and monetise our behaviour. The result is a hollowing out of deliberation: we decide less, and confirm more.

Some might argue that this is simply the cost of convenience—that users get what they want, and platforms are merely responding to demand. But this interpretation reverses the causal arrow. It assumes desire is fixed, rather than shaped. In reality, preference is malleable. Exposure begets familiarity; familiarity begets liking. The more we are shown a certain kind of product, aesthetic, or idea, the more inclined we are to view it as valuable or normal. This feedback loop blurs the line between what we choose and what we've been prepared to choose.

To be clear, technology does not eliminate freedom. It redefines its parameters. It exchanges one form of difficulty—navigating vast, unfiltered possibilities—for another: discerning when a "choice" is a true alternative and when it is merely a reinforced pattern. This redefinition matters because it alters the role of the user. Instead of an active agent navigating an open field, the user becomes a cursor moving within a structured frame, nudged along well-worn paths.

Recognising this shift is not an argument against digital systems, but an argument for greater awareness. We need not abandon platforms to reclaim agency. But we must interrogate the mechanisms through which choices are presented—and develop the literacy to distinguish between optionality and orchestration. When you are served a playlist, ask whether it reflects your tastes or simply extends your habits. When a product is placed at the top of a list, ask who paid for it to be there. When a decision feels effortless, consider what effort was avoided—and by whom.

The illusion of choice persists because it flatters us. It aligns with our self-image as discerning individuals, immune to manipulation. But in a world of predictive design and algorithmic curation, humility may be more useful than confidence. To act freely today requires not just the availability of options, but the awareness of how those options have been shaped—and a willingness, sometimes, to seek out what lies beyond the frame.

Comfort Is a System

The modern consumer rarely questions comfort. It arrives wrapped in ergonomic packaging, marketed as progress, delivered at the tap of a button. From pre-sorted playlists and food deliveries to algorithmically curated news and one-click purchases, convenience is sold not only as a lifestyle upgrade but as a default expectation. Yet beneath the frictionless surface lies a deeper truth: *comfort is not neutral.* It is built, structured, and distributed unevenly. It reflects choices—some visible, most concealed—made by designers, executives, and engineers whose incentives do not always align with the public good. Comfort, in short, is not merely a by-product of innovation; it is a system of power.

To understand how this system operates, we must first distinguish between convenience as an experience and comfort as an ideology. Convenience simplifies a task: ordering groceries from a phone rather than walking to the shop. Comfort, in its systematised form, normalises that simplification, encodes it into infrastructure, and embeds it into our habits and assumptions. What begins as a marginal improvement becomes, through repetition and scale, the new baseline. The initial moment of agency—choosing to use a tool—is gradually replaced by dependency on that tool's logic. We stop weighing the trade-off because the convenience now feels inevitable.

This inevitability is manufactured. The architecture of digital services is designed to present ease as both the path of least resistance and the only logical choice. When Google Maps defaults to the fastest route, most users take it without reflection, even if it diverts them through neighbourhoods or away from scenic detours. When Amazon offers one-day delivery, few pause to consider the logistics that enable that speed—or the labour practices behind it. The system works, so we trust it. But that trust often rests on what is unseen: the operational complexity, the environmental cost, the human toll.

Power is exercised in how these systems define effort, and whose effort counts. In the world of on-demand services, one person's comfort is often built upon another's invisible labour. The Uber passenger enjoys a seamless ride experience, while the driver absorbs the volatility of gig work, rated by an algorithm, paid per trip, monitored without recourse. The consumer of next-day delivery sees a clock counting down on their screen, but not the warehouse picker racing against it, nor the delivery driver skipping breaks to meet quota. The interface offers elegance; the system behind it extracts efficiency from those without leverage.

This asymmetry is not accidental—it is incentivised. The digital economy rewards businesses that can scale fast, reduce friction, and lock in habitual use. That reward structure drives design decisions that increasingly externalise discomfort: offloading complexity onto users with less power or embedding it in backend systems hidden from view. The most "frictionless" experiences are often those that have displaced friction elsewhere. Comfort, in this sense, is a resource—like energy or capital. And like any resource, it is distributed, contested, and political.

The market's pursuit of comfort frequently masks its ideological tilt. Take automation. When platforms automate tasks—auto-filling forms, recommending replies, or completing purchases—they reduce effort for the end user. But they also reshape cognition. Decisions that were once deliberate become reflexive. Engagement becomes passive. Over time, the skills we once exercised—navigating without GPS, comparing prices manually, writing without predictive text—atrophy. What's presented as a personal convenience is also a quiet redefinition of competence, nudging us away from effort as something meaningful and toward effortlessness as a goal.

Philosophically, this shift reveals a moral dimension to comfort that is often ignored. If every system optimises for ease, what happens to values that require difficulty—like deliberation, patience, or care? A society that pathologises inconvenience risks eroding the practices that sustain it. It treats friction not as a necessary condition for growth or resilience, but as a problem to be eliminated. Yet many of the capacities we prize—critical thinking, empathy, craftsmanship—emerge precisely through effort. They are built in the space that convenience seeks to collapse.

Designing systems that prioritise comfort often requires removing uncertainty, unpredictability, and ambiguity. But these are also the conditions in which learning and creativity flourish. When Spotify's algorithm decides your next song, or when Netflix autoplays your next episode, you're spared a decision—but also a moment of reflection, a possibility for surprise. The comfort is real, but so is the loss. The trade is subtle, but cumulative. Over time, we come to expect a world that anticipates our needs before we name them—and begin to distrust, or even resent, the situations that require navigation without guidance.

There is also a geopolitical dimension to the comfort system. The global platforms that dominate the convenience economy—Amazon, Google, Meta, Apple—are based in a handful of Western nations, yet they design products for billions of users worldwide. Their infrastructures shape expectations across cultures, often displacing local practices with global standards of usability and efficiency. What is intuitive in Silicon Valley becomes "universal" by default. In this way, the aesthetics of comfort carry cultural assumptions about what is desirable, normal, or worth preserving. Entire ways of doing—of relating, buying, remembering—are made obsolete not by lack of utility, but by lack of alignment with the system's logic.

To challenge this logic is not to reject comfort wholesale. Few would argue against technologies that genuinely reduce unnecessary hardship. But when convenience becomes the default measure of progress, we risk building systems that prize immediate ease over long-term agency. The core question becomes not "Does this make life easier?" but *"For whom, and at what cost?"* Comfort is a political artefact. It is a reflection of whose preferences are privileged, whose effort is minimised, and whose challenges are externalised or ignored.

Resisting the comfort system does not require abandoning digital tools, but it does require recalibrating our relationship to them. That begins with awareness. With recognising when friction has been removed not to empower us, but to extract from us—our data, our time, our attention. With learning to distinguish between what feels easy because it is well-designed, and what feels easy because it has eliminated the very conditions in which thoughtful choice can occur. And with remembering that the most meaningful forms of comfort—safety, dignity, connection—cannot be bought with a click. They are built, slowly, through systems of care, not just systems of speed.

In the end, the politics of comfort are not about rejecting luxury or aspiring to hardship. They are about refusing to accept ease as a proxy for good. They are about designing technologies that honour human complexity rather than erase it. They are about restoring friction where it protects values, and applying effort where it affirms dignity. And they are about understanding that what makes a system comfortable is not just how well it serves the user—but how justly it treats the world beyond the screen.

Chapter 2
Memory, Outsourced

We once carried more within our own minds. Not because we were exceptionally gifted or trained to remember, but because memory was necessity, not choice. It formed the quiet scaffolding of daily life—an invisible network that held our days together. We remembered telephone numbers, the rhythm of streets, our relatives' birthdays, the ingredients of a meal. We remembered where we parked, when a bill was due, what a conversation implied. It wasn't something to be proud of; it was simply how one lived. Now, those same fragments of life reside elsewhere—on devices, in search histories, digital calendars, satellite maps. We didn't declare an intent to forget; we just found ourselves unburdened by the need to hold things in mind.

This chapter is about that unspoken migration of memory from the mind to the machine. It isn't nostalgia for pre-digital days, nor a plea for their return. Rather, it's an attempt to trace what's quietly changed—psychologically, culturally, neurologically—when remembering becomes optional. As our devices store more for us, the nature of attention shifts. So too does the way we assign importance, the manner in which we maintain identity over time. Memory, after all, isn't just data retrieval; it's a signal of care, a measure of meaning, and the ground from which agency grows.

Take, for instance, our sense of place. Before the blue dot of GPS began leading the way, navigating a city meant engaging the body and brain together. You remembered corners, turns, landmarks. You learned patterns in distance and direction, and slowly built an internal map that was both practical and personal. Today, that faculty has atrophied for many. We follow instructions rather than constructing understanding. Studies in *Nature Communications* reveal reduced hippocampal activity in habitual GPS users—the very area responsible for spatial navigation and memory. The principle is familiar: use it, or lose it. More and more, we are choosing the latter.

This isn't only about neural circuits; it's about the experience of being somewhere. To know where you are is also to sense how places connect. That relational awareness gives rise to curiosity, adaptability, and even a kind of freedom. When navigation is outsourced, movement becomes efficient but empty—you arrive, but you don't *learn* the way. The journey delivers location, not knowledge.

Personal memory tells a similar story. Many of us can no longer recall our friends' numbers by heart, nor birthdays without a prompt. It seems a small price for convenience. Yet when we allow machines to remember on our behalf, something subtler erodes: the meaning embedded in the act of recollection itself. Remembering is a form of regard. It says, "You matter enough for me to hold you in mind." When we forget because we no longer need to remember, we delegate that regard as well.

The same holds true in intimacy. The unprompted recollection of a shared detail—a song, a passing remark, a private joke—communicates a kind of presence no notification can replicate. Technology can remind us *that* a birthday exists; it cannot re-create the significance of remembering it unaided. Devices may store, but they do not remember. That distinction, subtle though it seems, accumulates meaning over time.

Psychologists call one aspect of this the "Google Effect." First described by Betsy Sparrow and colleagues at Columbia University, it captures how we tend to forget information we expect to find again easily. When knowledge becomes instantly retrievable, we cease to embed it in memory. It's a clever adaptation, perhaps, but also a quiet transformation in how we learn and value what we know. Retrieval replaces reflection; access stands in for understanding.

The consequences ripple through education, work, and thought itself. Learning once required effort—the labour of turning knowledge into something inward. Now, the distinction between *knowing* and *being able to look up* has blurred. The student who can summon facts at speed may still lack the deeper comprehension that once came from holding ideas in mind. The professional whose expertise lives in databases is, in truth, dependent upon them. Distributed cognition can be powerful, yes—but it's fragile too. The moment access falters, the illusion of mastery disappears.

We often describe this shift as liberation: freedom from the drudgery of memorisation, from cluttered minds. And there is relief in that. But rarely do we consider what the labour of remembering once did *for* us. To remember is to choose—to decide that something deserves to endure. When machines make that decision for us, we surrender a small, persistent form of authorship over our own inner world.

Because memory is not only practical—it is constitutive. Who we are depends on what we recall and how we connect those recollections. Our inner narratives are stitched from remembered details: faces, places, failures, triumphs. When these are scattered across cloud servers and platforms, fragmented into notifications and photo feeds, our sense of self becomes harder to thread together. We may become curators of our archives, yet less fluent in the story they tell.

And let's not pretend the digital archive is impartial. It remembers selectively. Platforms preserve what is photogenic or profitable, what can be measured or monetised. Search engines privilege what's recent or popular; reminders privilege what's urgent. Meaning is rarely part of the algorithmic equation. So, what is externalised is already filtered—not through our priorities, but through those of the system. We recall what we are nudged to recall.

All of this brings us back to autonomy. When remembering becomes something triggered by a ping rather than summoned by will, we lose a quiet but profound power—the ability to decide what matters. The act of voluntary recollection anchors us in ourselves; it affirms continuity between past and present. To surrender that habit entirely is to risk becoming porous to the designs of the tools we depend on.

Yet the solution is not renunciation. The task is subtler: to preserve conscious remembering within a landscape designed for forgetting. To choose, occasionally, to carry something in mind when you could as easily offload it. To hold a number, a date, a phrase not because you must, but because it connects you to someone or something you value.

Perhaps this, then, is the quiet invitation of our time: to notice what we've stopped remembering, and to decide—deliberately—what we wish to keep. Because in the end, what we remember marks the contour of what we care about. And what we no longer do might tell us, with unnerving precision, what we've allowed to slip from significance.

The Decline of Mental Maps

For most of human history, knowing where you were was a matter of survival. Whether traversing the open sea, navigating through dense forest, or threading a path through unfamiliar city streets, our ability to orient ourselves, recall landmarks, and form mental maps of our surroundings was not a luxury but a cognitive necessity. Today, this ancient skillset is rapidly fading—not through natural evolution, but through technological substitution. Global Positioning System (GPS) tools have become so embedded in everyday life that many people now rely on them reflexively, even in familiar environments. The cost of this convenience, however, is not just the loss of self-reliant navigation. It is a measurable decline in a key region of the brain—and a fundamental shift in how we relate to space, place, and memory itself.

Spatial navigation is primarily governed by the hippocampus, a structure buried deep within the brain's medial temporal lobe. The hippocampus plays a vital role in encoding spatial information, forming long-term memories, and constructing what neuroscientists call "cognitive maps"—internal models of the external world that allow us to orient ourselves, visualise routes, and imagine spatial relationships. When we navigate using our own faculties—recalling turns, noticing landmarks, mentally calculating direction—we engage the hippocampus in dynamic and sustained ways. But when we follow step-by-step instructions from a screen, that engagement is significantly reduced.

A landmark study published in *The Journal of Neuroscience* in 2017, conducted by neuroscientists at University College London, found that participants using GPS-like instructions to navigate virtual environments showed no measurable activity in the hippocampus or prefrontal cortex. In contrast, those who explored freely and chose their own paths demonstrated robust activation in both regions. In short, when we stop navigating, we stop exercising the parts of the brain responsible for doing so. And like any underused muscle, those regions begin to weaken. In real-world terms, this means that habitual reliance on GPS may lead not only to poorer navigation skills, but to long-term structural and functional changes in the brain.

This is not speculative. Research comparing taxi drivers in London—who must memorise thousands of streets and routes for "The Knowledge" licensing exam—with control groups has shown that their posterior hippocampi are significantly larger. The longer they have been driving, the greater the enlargement. This anatomical change reflects a simple principle: the brain adapts to demand. Remove the demand, and the adaptation reverses. The hippocampus, it seems, is as plastic as it is essential.

Yet the implications of the decline in mental mapping are not limited to geography. Wayfinding is more than finding your way—it is an act of attention, judgment, problem-solving, and orientation in both physical and conceptual space. When we navigate manually, we are not just recalling landmarks; we are evaluating scale, estimating distance, noticing environmental cues, and making directional decisions in real time. This fosters a form of situated awareness that is active, embodied, and attentive. By contrast, GPS systems convert space into data and decision-making into obedience. The user no longer asks, "Where am I in relation to X?" but rather, "What does the voice tell me to do next?"

The psychological impact is equally significant. Human beings have long used spatial memory as an organising framework for knowledge. Memory palaces, an ancient mnemonic device dating back to Classical antiquity, use imagined spaces to store and retrieve information. Our brains are spatial by nature. The act of navigating through a city, or even through a building, reinforces a sense of continuity and embodied presence. It creates mental scaffolding on which we hang memories, stories, and meanings. The decline of this activity does not merely affect our ability to get from one place to another—it undermines a cognitive system we have depended on for millennia.

One of the most consequential effects of GPS dependency is the erosion of environmental engagement. The more we rely on digital systems to guide us, the less we attend to the physical world. A person guided by GPS may not notice the street names, the character of a neighbourhood, the direction of the sun, or even the location of key landmarks. They are following instructions, not building understanding. This passivity dulls not just spatial skills but perceptual sensitivity.

The richness of place—the way it looks, smells, sounds, and feels—becomes background noise to the calculated route.

Moreover, GPS does not just *replace* mental mapping; it subtly *reorients* our relationship to time and space. Routes are evaluated not for beauty, interest, or significance, but for efficiency. "Fastest route" becomes the de facto objective, marginalising detours, spontaneous exploration, or getting pleasantly lost. The goal becomes arrival, not experience. This transactional framing of movement is particularly striking in urban settings, where digital navigation tools have reshaped not only how people move, but why. The journey is no longer a spatial narrative; it is an optimisation problem.

This technocentric approach to navigation also has infrastructural consequences. Cities are increasingly designed around vehicles guided by data, rather than people guided by perception. As smart routing becomes ubiquitous, traffic flows are redistributed in ways that prioritise efficiency over human-scale engagement. Neighbourhoods once quiet may become clogged as GPS systems route drivers through side streets to avoid congestion. Individuals may follow routes that make no spatial sense to them, but which satisfy the algorithm's logic. The city becomes legible not to its inhabitants, but to its systems.

There is a deeper philosophical tension here between embodied knowing and delegated knowing. When we know a place ourselves—when we can walk it in our minds, describe it to others, adapt when conditions change—we possess a kind of cognitive sovereignty. We are not just passengers in space, but participants in it. GPS systems, by contrast, promise liberation from the burden of memory and the friction of uncertainty. They deliver, with remarkable accuracy, a kind of prosthetic knowing: outsourced, efficient, and non-reflective. But this very convenience risks de-skilling us. We become dependent on systems we do not understand and cannot replicate if they fail.

This dependency is rarely questioned, because the technology works so well. GPS systems are astonishing feats of engineering—blending satellite triangulation, real-time traffic data, and predictive modelling to deliver precise guidance. Their utility is undeniable. The problem arises when that utility becomes habitual, and the habit becomes structural. The transition from help to reliance is gradual, subtle, and largely invisible. But the effect is cumulative: fewer people can navigate unaided, fewer develop a working knowledge of their environments, and fewer pass on those skills to others.

Importantly, this decline is not evenly distributed. Age, geography, education, and socioeconomic status all influence how navigation skills are learned and maintained. In places where GPS is inaccessible or unreliable, traditional wayfinding persists. In cultures where oral directions, landmark-based navigation, or collective memory remain strong, spatial skills are still transmitted across generations. But these are increasingly exceptions to a rule being written in code.

To reverse or even mitigate this trend requires more than nostalgic appeals to "figure it out yourself." It requires recognising the value of spatial cognition—not just as a practical skill, but as a cognitive and cultural asset. Parents teaching children how to read a map. Educators using navigation tasks to build memory and resilience. Urban planners designing environments that reward exploration rather than optimise throughput. These are not acts of resistance; they are acts of recovery—restoring capacities that quietly anchor our relationship to the world.

Ultimately, the decline of mental maps is not about forgetting directions—it is about forgetting how to locate ourselves without external instruction. In a landscape saturated with guidance, the ability to chart your own course—literally and figuratively—becomes a rarer and more radical act. Navigation, once a ubiquitous human faculty, is at risk of becoming a niche skill, relegated to hobbyists, adventurers, or those without access to digital aids. If that happens, we will not just have lost a method of wayfinding. We will have forfeited a foundational piece of how we engage with space, remember the world, and think for ourselves.

Numbers We Used to Know

There was a time—not long ago—when most people could recall a dozen phone numbers by heart. Parents' landlines, friends' extensions, the local taxi rank, your partner's number scrawled in your mind as firmly as on paper. Today, for many, it is difficult to recall even one. The digits have not disappeared; they've migrated. They now live in devices, silently stored and instantly retrieved. But in outsourcing this once-routine act of remembering, something subtle but significant has been lost—not just a function, but a form of familiarity. Memory is not merely a technical operation. It is a marker of value, intimacy, and personal commitment. When we stop remembering certain things, we begin, quietly, to signal that they no longer require remembering.

The externalisation of memory is often framed as a gain—of efficiency, of reliability, of bandwidth. And it's true: digital address books are faster, more comprehensive, and less error-prone than our fallible minds. Yet the transition from internal to external storage marks more than a change in medium. It shifts the *burden* of remembering from the self to the system, and in doing so, reconfigures the meaning of what we remember in the first place. Knowing a phone number used to be more than a utility; it was a declaration of care. You didn't remember just because you had to. You remembered because it mattered.

This is not a sentimental point. It is a cognitive and social one. Embedded memory—the kind stored in the mind rather than a device—shapes not only how we act, but how we relate. When you recall someone's number, birthday, or anniversary without prompting, you demonstrate attention. You show that the person occupies cognitive real estate without needing to be summoned. That act builds trust, closeness, and a shared sense of relevance. It says, *I carry you with me, even when you're not in front of me.* A notification can simulate the behaviour—prompting a call, sending a reminder—but it cannot replicate the meaning behind it. The emotional charge comes not from the action alone, but from its provenance.

The psychological architecture behind this shift is well documented. Memory researchers distinguish between *semantic* memory (facts, general knowledge) and *episodic* memory (personal experiences). The move to digital storage affects both, but most acutely targets what might be termed *relational memory*: those details we remember specifically because of who they connect us to. This includes not just numbers and dates, but preferences, routines, habits—small things we retain to show we've been paying attention. Digital tools are excellent at collecting such data, but remembering them ourselves is how we demonstrate presence.

This distinction matters in a world increasingly defined by ambient computing and predictive systems. A contact's birthday may be flagged by Facebook or your calendar, prompting a message that appears thoughtful but was, in fact, machine-initiated. A partner's coffee order may be remembered by a loyalty app, not by the person ordering. These substitutions are functionally effective but relationally shallow. When an expression of care is entirely mediated by an external system, the *perception* of intention is diluted. The result is not only a decline in memory practice, but a subtle erosion of interpersonal meaning.

There is also a cognitive trade-off at work. The act of remembering reinforces memory; the act of offloading bypasses that reinforcement. Psychologist Daniel Wegner, in his work on *transactive memory*, argued that individuals in close relationships often divide cognitive labour—each remembering different details, relying on the other as a mental extension. This is healthy and adaptive within human networks. But when the transactive partner becomes a device, the relationship is asymmetrical. The device never forgets, but neither does it engage in mutual recall. It does not *know* what it remembers. The human becomes less active, more dependent, and potentially less confident in their own memory capacities.

This dependency becomes particularly striking when digital access is disrupted. Ask yourself: without your phone, how many numbers could you dial? How many addresses could you find? How many birthdays could you recall unprompted? In extreme cases—such as power outages, travel disruptions, or device failures—what was intended as assistance becomes a point of vulnerability. The skill was never truly transferred; it was decommissioned. The memory is not dormant—it's absent.

The long-term implications are not yet fully understood, but early studies suggest that habitual reliance on external memory systems can alter how the brain encodes and retrieves information. Researchers have observed that when people expect to have future access to information—via Google, for instance—they are less likely to remember the information itself, and more likely to remember where to find it. This adaptive strategy may be efficient, but it also shifts the locus of cognitive authority away from the self. The brain becomes a map to external storage rather than a storehouse in its own right.

This shift is reinforced by interface design. Contacts apps do not encourage recall; they render it unnecessary. Calendar reminders don't merely jog memory; they replace it. Voice assistants execute commands without requiring retention. The affordances of these tools promote a model of cognition that privileges access over ownership. We no longer know; we retrieve. This is not an indictment—it is a description. But it raises a critical question: *What happens to the parts of ourselves we used to keep in mind, and now no longer do?*

One effect is a narrowing of spontaneous thought. When everything important is scheduled, stored, and searchable, we leave less room for associative recall—for the moments when a name, a date, or a number rises unbidden and reorients our attention. These mental intrusions, far from being distractions, are often how reflection and insight occur. Memory is not merely a bank. It is a trigger system, surfacing things that matter without being asked. When that system is outsourced, we may become more efficient—but also more linear, more mechanical, less capable of drifting toward meaning through remembered connection.

There is a temptation to dismiss these concerns as trivial. So what if we no longer remember phone numbers? Isn't that precisely what technology is for—to relieve us of menial burdens? The answer depends on how we define "menial." If remembering a birthday or a phone number is purely instrumental, then offloading it is rational. But if it is also symbolic—if it signals care, attention, or identity—then forgetting carries a social and emotional cost. The meaning of the remembered detail is not in its content, but in its custody.

This tension—between efficiency and intimacy, between offloading and retaining—reflects a broader cultural recalibration. The tools we use shape not just how we act, but what we believe is worth doing ourselves. When a phone remembers everything for us, we slowly cease to ask whether we still *want* to remember, or what it might mean if we did. Over time, remembering becomes optional, even eccentric. Yet to remember is, fundamentally, to say: *this mattered enough to keep.*

Reclaiming memory, then, is not a rejection of technology but a reassertion of its limits. It is a reminder that not all remembering is about necessity—some is about presence, ritual, and respect. We may never again memorise long lists of numbers, nor should we. But we might choose, deliberately, to remember one or two that matter. Not because we need to, but because *someone* needs to know they are held in mind. And because memory, when it is chosen rather than imposed, is one of the most human acts still available to us.

Google Brain

It is now possible to forget without consequence. Type a half-remembered phrase into a search engine, and the answer appears within seconds. The date of a historical event, the name of an obscure theory, a forgotten actor in a decades-old film—these details no longer need to be stored in the mind, because they are perpetually available elsewhere. This ambient access to information has changed not only how we search, but how we remember—and more importantly, how we *expect* to remember. The brain, faced with a world in which knowledge is one click away, is reorganising itself around that assumption. What emerges is a new cognitive landscape—distributed, dependent, and quietly reshaped by design.

The term *Google Effect* was coined by psychologist Betsy Sparrow and her colleagues in a 2011 study published in *Science*, which found that people are less likely to remember information if they believe it will be readily accessible later. Crucially, they tend instead to remember *where* to find it. The effect is subtle but profound: the brain is shifting from storing content to storing location. Memory becomes less about the fact itself and more about the path to the fact. This isn't laziness—it's adaptation. Faced with an environment saturated by retrievable information, the brain economises. It assumes what's externally available does not need internal redundancy.

This behavioural shift parallels changes in information architecture. The way digital systems are designed—indexed, searchable, persistent—reinforces the habit of external recall.

A person might forget the details of a news article, knowing they can re-Google the headline. A student may recall the source of an academic concept without recalling the concept itself. This creates a kind of cognitive outsourcing that is functional in the short term but increasingly alters the relationship between knowledge and identity. If the self is partly constituted by what we know and how we integrate it, what happens when that knowing is continually deferred?

At one level, the Google Effect appears to make sense. It's arguably irrational to memorise things that are universally and instantly accessible. Why clutter mental space with facts that can be retrieved more efficiently from an external source? Yet the value of memory is not in redundancy alone—it's in synthesis. Memorised knowledge is not inert data. It forms the foundation for reasoning, intuition, and creativity. When we carry facts with us, we can juxtapose them, draw analogies, test hypotheses without switching contexts. This is what psychologists call *working knowledge*—information actively available for cognitive processing, not just stored externally like a filing cabinet.

The danger is not in the act of looking up, but in the habit of never encoding. Learning becomes shallow when it is decoupled from retention. This distinction is critical in education, where understanding requires more than exposure. It requires the mental scaffolding that allows new information to be anchored to what is already known. When learners rely too heavily on lookup culture, they fail to develop these scaffolds. They become fluent in retrieval but brittle in reasoning. They may perform well on fact-based assessments but struggle with integration, problem-solving, or conceptual transfer.

This has implications beyond the classroom. In professional settings, the assumption that knowledge is always externally available can breed a dependence that impairs decision-making. A surgeon who forgets a protocol cannot Google mid-operation. A negotiator who loses thread in a complex discussion cannot pause for a search. Expertise, in such domains, is not just about access to facts—it is about fluency, judgment, and recall under pressure. These are functions of memory, not of storage.

There is also a social dimension to the Google Effect. When everyone relies on the same search engines, the architecture of information retrieval becomes a gatekeeper. Algorithms decide what is surfaced first, what is buried, what is framed as authoritative. Users often confuse availability with reliability, forgetting that search results are ranked by engagement, profitability, or click-through rates—not by epistemic weight. This creates a collective vulnerability: if memory is displaced by search, and search is shaped by opaque systems, then public knowledge is increasingly susceptible to manipulation.

This is not a hypothetical concern. Studies of misinformation show that users are more likely to remember *false* claims they encounter repeatedly, even when corrected. Moreover, repeated exposure through search or social platforms can make those claims feel more familiar, and therefore more true—a phenomenon known as the *illusory truth effect*. When we stop holding knowledge ourselves and rely on fluid, externally curated streams, we become passive participants in our own cognition. The very act of remembering is no longer anchored in experience, but in whatever content is most visible at the moment of retrieval.

Philosophically, this shift forces a reconsideration of what it means to know something. Is knowledge the ability to recall from within, or the ability to access on demand? If the former, then the Google Effect represents a decline in intellectual sovereignty. If the latter, then knowledge becomes a logistical problem—no longer a matter of cultivation, but of connectivity. This view aligns with some theories in cognitive science, such as *extended mind* theory, which argues that tools like notebooks, devices, and even other people can function as parts of our cognitive system. But even this model requires intentional engagement. A tool is only an extension of the mind if it is deliberately integrated. The casual act of Googling, over time, can become automatic, unconscious, and unreflective.

What complicates matters is that the brain itself is highly plastic. It will adapt to prevailing modes of interaction. Just as literate societies developed different neural patterns from oral ones, digitally saturated societies are developing new mental habits—habits shaped by interruption, fragmentation, and search-driven thinking. The shift is not inherently negative, but it demands scrutiny. What are we optimising for? Speed? Surface-level coverage? Cognitive offloading? And what are we sacrificing—depth, synthesis, long-term retention?

Some argue that these changes are simply the next step in human evolution. Just as writing externalised oral memory, and printing externalised textual preservation, so too does search externalise declarative knowledge. But this analogy misses an important distinction. Prior revolutions in memory technology still required the user to engage deeply with content—writing, copying, annotating. Digital retrieval, by contrast, encourages skimming, scanning, and transience. The tools do not demand attention; they encourage acceleration.

This acceleration affects not only what we remember but *how we experience knowledge*. There is a qualitative difference between remembering a fact because it shaped your thinking and re-encountering it endlessly through hyperlinks. The former anchors you; the latter orbits you. One builds identity. The other builds dependence.

To respond meaningfully to the Google Effect requires more than digital hygiene. It calls for reintroducing friction into our learning processes—deliberate recall, spaced repetition, active summarisation. It means treating memory not as a liability, but as an investment in autonomy. This is particularly urgent in a world where information is abundant, but coherence is scarce.

The point is not to memorise everything, nor to deny the utility of search. It is to reclaim the *choice* of remembering. To resist the automatic assumption that anything worth knowing can be re-Googled. To develop intellectual habits that honour the value of holding knowledge internally—not because we have to, but because doing so keeps us present, connected, and capable of thought that isn't outsourced before it begins. In a culture of lookup, deliberate memory is a quiet form of resistance—and perhaps, more than that, a practice of intellectual care.

What We Stop Practicing

There is no alert that sounds when a cognitive skill begins to atrophy. No notification informs us that something we once did fluently is slowly slipping out of reach. The decline is quiet, distributed across unremarkable days, woven into the convenience of delegation. One by one, we stop recalling birthdays because the calendar pings them. We stop navigating familiar routes because a screen narrates them. We stop remembering details of conversations because they're archived in chat logs. What begins as a helpful extension becomes a silent erosion. *The brain adapts not only to what it does, but to what it no longer needs to do.*

Cognitive offloading—shifting mental tasks to external aids—is not inherently problematic. Humans have always used tools to expand memory: knots tied for reminders, books for storage, computers for data. But what distinguishes today's offloading is its pervasiveness, invisibility, and speed. We no longer make a conscious choice to remember or not; we default to devices by design. And when remembering is no longer practised, it ceases to function as a meaningful act. It becomes vestigial.

The consequences of this are not merely technical—they are deeply personal and philosophical. What we remember shapes what we pay attention to. And what we pay attention to shapes who we believe we are. Memory, in this context, is not a passive archive but an active agent. It informs how we prioritise, how we behave, how we relate to others. When the act of remembering is bypassed, attention is rerouted. We begin to focus not on content but on access. The question shifts from *what do I know?* to *how fast can I retrieve it?*

This shift has tangible effects on attention. Practising memory requires sustained mental effort: repetition, visualisation, emotional association. It asks the mind to hold and integrate. By contrast, lookup culture fragments attention. It replaces depth with interruption, turns recall into reaction, and discourages lingering with information. Over time, the absence of mental rehearsal reduces our capacity to focus. The brain, shaped by its routines, starts to expect external scaffolding. And attention, once sharpened by the labour of remembering, is dulled by reliance.

But the decline is not simply about performance—it is about valuation. Remembering is a form of honouring. We remember what we care about. When we stop remembering something, we risk signalling, however unintentionally, that it no longer matters. Forgetting your friend's birthday because the platform didn't remind you might be excusable. But if it happens often enough, the message received is not about the platform—it's about the relationship. Memory, in human terms, is more than a mechanism. It is a gesture of regard.

This becomes more pronounced in interpersonal relationships. Consider a partner who remembers your coffee order, your favourite film, your father's name. These details are not critical—they can all be stored and retrieved. But when they are remembered *unprompted*, they carry weight. They say, *I paid attention. I kept this with me.* The shift to outsourcing these details—whether to apps, shared calendars, or AI assistants—may keep things running, but it also strips these acts of their intentionality. The memory still exists, but it no longer travels through the person.

There is also a broader identity cost. The self is built from memory—not just autobiographical memory, but procedural and semantic memory as well. Knowing how to do things, remembering why they matter, holding fragments of the past that inform the present—these are the scaffolds of identity. When fewer of those fragments are actively held, the narrative coherence of the self can thin. A person who cannot recall past decisions, who does not carry forward internalised knowledge, begins to experience life more as reaction than as continuity.

This has ramifications for how we learn, how we relate, and how we construct meaning. In educational contexts, the decline in memory practice has led to a pedagogy overly reliant on exposure and retrieval, rather than internalisation. Students who can Google an answer may not remember the concept an hour later. Professionals who depend on searchable archives may lose intuitive fluency in their field. The illusion of knowing replaces the reality of integration. This is not a failure of intelligence; it is the predictable result of unpractised retention.

Some might argue that as long as we know *where* to find the information, there's no need to carry it internally. But this view underestimates the difference between knowledge and access. Knowing something means being able to summon it in context, to connect it to other ideas, to apply it under pressure. Accessing something, by contrast, is contingent. It requires the right conditions, the right tools, the right prompts. It is vulnerable to interruption, distortion, or delay. And it does not build cognitive flexibility.

Moreover, the act of practising memory builds more than retention—it builds autonomy. When we rely less on external cues, we cultivate internal reference points. We become less reactive, more grounded, more capable of sustained thought. This matters not only for personal development but for civic life. A society in which memory is consistently outsourced is one in which citizens may struggle to remember the details of public policy, the patterns of history, the promises of leaders. They become susceptible to narrative manipulation, because they lack the internalised benchmarks to evaluate what they are told. *Memory is not just personal competence—it is civic infrastructure.*

The practice of memory also supports resilience. To remember how you solved a problem, how you endured difficulty, how you learned from failure—these recollections equip you for future challenges. When those experiences are not encoded—because they were outsourced, recorded but not retained—they cannot serve this function. The result is a shallower engagement with life's lessons. We may have the record, but not the insight.

And yet, despite these costs, the drift continues—largely unnoticed, largely unresisted. The reason is simple: delegation feels easier. Remembering takes effort, and modern systems are engineered to remove effort wherever possible. Interfaces nudge us to forget, to let go, to "set and forget." But when we comply too often, the forgetting becomes permanent. What we stop practising becomes what we can no longer do.

Reintroducing memory practice into daily life is neither radical nor nostalgic. It is restorative. It begins with small acts: memorising a phone number, recalling a quote without searching, testing recall before resorting to notes. These are not performative exercises—they are recalibrations of attention. They remind us that remembering is not about resisting progress, but about preserving agency. In choosing to remember, we affirm value. We decide what matters enough to be carried with us.

We live in an age of abundance—of data, of access, of reminders. But abundance without selectivity leads to overload, not clarity. Practised memory offers a filter—not just for information, but for meaning. It says: *this, I will hold myself.* It is a quiet declaration of responsibility, attention, and care. And in a culture that incentivises forgetting, it may be one of the most enduring forms of presence we have left.

Chapter 3
The Death of Getting Lost

To be lost is to meet the world without a script—to move through space with nothing but instinct, attention, and the willingness to decide before knowing. Disorientation, though it carries a hint of danger in its name, has always been a doorway to discovery. When we lose our bearings, our senses flare awake; the world feels newly alive, its details insistent, its possibilities multiplied. Yet in our age of relentless optimisation, that state of unknowing has been carefully designed out of existence. GPS, real-time maps, predictive routing, recommendation engines—each works to keep us on track, to ensure no turn goes unanticipated. We are always "on course," and so, paradoxically, we no longer *travel* in the full sense of the word. Efficiency has replaced exploration; precision has eclipsed presence. By making it impossible to lose our way, we have quietly lost something more profound: the art of truly encountering place.

What follows is an inquiry into that disappearance—into what fades from experience when we no longer allow ourselves, or are no longer able, to get lost. The argument stretches beyond geography; it touches creativity, thought, and social life. As our dependence on digital guidance deepens, the way we move through cities changes, as does the way we think about space and time. Our tools, designed to orient us, are also shaping how we perceive. We follow the path but stop seeing the terrain. The device dictates direction, and in return, the world becomes a backdrop—flattened, navigable, but less alive.

This transformation is most visible in the small acts of daily movement. Once, crossing a city meant remembering. You carried a mental map, tracing routes, noticing landmarks, correcting small errors through improvisation. Now, it is a sequence of instructions: a glowing arrow, a robotic voice, a confirmation beep. The convenience feels harmless, even generous. Yet over time, it quietly shrinks our cognitive reach. Studies have found that habitual GPS users show diminished activity in the hippocampus—the brain's centre for spatial reasoning and memory. The more faithfully we follow, the less we remember. The journey remains visible to the device, but becomes invisible to the mind.

This erosion of spatial memory reshapes not only how we move, but how we *inhabit* our environments. Cities, once stitched together by memory, myth, and happenstance, now appear as neatly parcelled grids of function and access. The emerging "smart city" promises seamlessness: adaptive lighting, predictive transport, sensor-based infrastructure. Yet in smoothing out friction, it also erases the rough textures through which curiosity grows. Gone is the necessity of asking for directions, of stumbling across an unfamiliar street, of being surprised by what you didn't seek. The city becomes a system to be used, not a place to be known.

Time, too, has been reprogrammed. Travel once offered intervals of mental idleness—those slow, transitional moments on a bus or a platform when thought wandered freely. Now, these pockets of pause are filled with feeds, messages, and curated content. Our attention, instead of expanding outward, contracts toward the screen. Movement has ceased to be an opportunity for reflection; it has become another form of occupation. We are rarely still, but also rarely *present*.

The deeper loss here is not just navigational skill but wayfinding—a subtle distinction worth preserving. Navigation is about efficiency, about moving from point to point with minimal error. Wayfinding, by contrast, is an act of interpretation. It involves reading the environment, engaging memory, intuition, and curiosity. It's the difference between being guided and *guiding yourself.* Wayfinding has ancient roots: it connects us to the migratory habits of our ancestors, to the oral geographies of Indigenous cultures where knowing the land meant understanding one's own place within it. To lose this is not just to lose a mental faculty—it is to forfeit a worldview.

When we no longer get lost, we also lose the conditions for serendipity. Detours, chance discoveries, the small accidents that give journeys their texture—all are casualties of optimisation. The shortest route leaves no room for surprise. Every recalculation promises to correct deviation, not celebrate it. Over time, this cultivates a subtle obedience. The map says go left; we go left. The algorithm knows best. We follow not because we must, but because it feels natural to do so. What disappears in this process is the quiet thrill of uncertainty—the alertness that comes from not quite knowing where you are, but trusting yourself to find out.

Behind this lies a psychology of control. Modern systems are designed to soothe our discomfort with unpredictability. Every estimated arrival time, every progress bar, every "rerouting" announcement is a small assurance that chaos has been tamed. Yet control has its costs. In relinquishing the right to be lost, we surrender the muscle of improvisation. The traveller becomes an operator, executing instructions. Agency shifts from the human to the system, and with it, a subtle aspect of freedom slips away.

To be lost, then, is not to fail. It is to enter a state of openness—an interval where the familiar loosens and the unexpected steps forward. It is a moment that demands attention and rewards it in kind. In losing our way, we find new ways of seeing, thinking, and sometimes even being. The discomfort of disorientation can give rise to perspective, to humility, to wonder. It reminds us that the world was never built solely for our convenience—and that this is precisely what makes it worth exploring.

None of this suggests that digital navigation must be abandoned. Its benefits are undeniable. But to rely on it exclusively is to impoverish the self. Perhaps the challenge now is not to delete the map, but to step away from it often enough to remember what it means to find our bearings unaided. To recover wayfinding as an act of attention, of curiosity, of trust in one's own capacity to orient within complexity. Getting lost, in this sense, is not about losing direction at all—it is about reclaiming it. In learning again to wander without certainty, we might rediscover something stubbornly human: the thrill of presence in a world not yet entirely known.

From Exploration to Execution

A map, once a symbol of uncertainty and possibility, has become a symbol of certainty. The shift is profound but deceptively quiet: from reading our environment to following instructions; from discovering space to executing routes. The rise of digital navigation tools—from GPS apps to algorithmically optimised journey planners—has turned the once-intricate task of finding our way into a streamlined process of getting from A to B with maximum efficiency. While this has undeniably improved convenience and accessibility, it has also transformed the cognitive and emotional texture of movement itself. *We no longer wander—we comply*. We no longer ask where we are—we are told. And in the process, we have lost a form of active engagement with the world that shaped how we understood it.

Wandering was never just inefficient navigation. It was a mode of attention. A way of being attuned to place, possibility, and surprise. When people used to set out without precise instructions, they depended on an evolving relationship with their environment. They noticed subtle landmarks, adjusted for intuition, and tolerated ambiguity. Being slightly unsure was not only acceptable—it was expected. Today, this tolerance has withered. Apps like Google Maps, Waze, and

Apple Maps have recalibrated expectations around travel. Precision is now the norm, and deviation feels like a glitch. This subtle reframing has behavioural consequences: we now *fear* getting lost. We interpret unscripted movement as inefficient or irresponsible. The comfort of knowing where we are at all times has supplanted the cognitive resilience that once emerged from not knowing.

The effects of this shift go beyond navigation. They extend into how we experience our surroundings—and how much of those surroundings we actually perceive. By focusing narrowly on turn-by-turn directions, our peripheral awareness shrinks. Research in cognitive psychology has repeatedly shown that attentional focus is a limited resource: when we concentrate intensely on one thing (e.g., following a blue dot on a screen), we filter out everything else. This is a classic case of inattentional blindness, where what we don't notice isn't just irrelevant detail—it's often the texture of lived experience. A shopfront glimpsed out of the corner of the eye, an alley that leads somewhere unexpected, a building that evokes memory or curiosity—these moments vanish when our attention is locked onto executing a planned route.

The irony is that our digital tools were never designed to enhance discovery. They were designed to optimise travel. Every route is a problem to be solved: the fastest, shortest, most direct path. But exploration is not a problem to be solved. It is a form of openness to what cannot be predicted. And this distinction matters. When we switch from *exploring* to *executing*, we shift from participatory engagement to passive compliance. We stop asking questions of the space around us—Where does that lead? What's down there? Who built that?—and instead become preoccupied with the confirmation that we are on the correct trajectory. Even microdecisions—left or right, pause or continue, cross here or there—are no longer ours to make. They've been pre-decided by software that has modelled what matters, often without our awareness of its criteria.

These criteria are not neutral. They are built on assumptions about what is valuable: speed, convenience, avoidance of traffic or uncertainty. Apps do not ask whether you'd like to take the scenic route, encounter something beautiful, or be pleasantly delayed by a bookshop. They assume such possibilities are inefficient and thus undesirable. This is optimisation logic at its core—flattening the landscape of travel into metrics. A ten-minute walk becomes a data point to be minimised, rather than an opportunity for encounter. And with every iteration of these tools, we become more fluent in the logic they impose and less fluent in the sensory and emotional language of place.

Historically, getting lost was not only a rite of passage but a source of knowledge. Cities were once deciphered by walking. In the flâneur tradition of 19th-century Paris, wandering was a political and aesthetic act—a way of claiming space and finding meaning within it. Even in recent decades, many of us remember the quiet satisfaction of piecing together a new area over repeated visits, mapping it slowly in our heads. Today, we often revisit places without ever really knowing where we've been. Our memory is scaffolded not by paths walked and turns made but by search histories and past destinations in apps. The city ceases to be a legible surface and becomes a set of coordinates: destinations without context, spaces without stories.

The problem is not the presence of digital navigation, but its dominance. We've allowed execution to overwrite exploration as the default mode of movement. This has implications not only for individuals but for urban design, social behaviour, and collective imagination. If people stop moving unpredictably through cities, cities become less responsive to spontaneous needs. If every movement is purposeful, places that exist to be stumbled upon—small galleries, side cafés, hidden gardens—lose their audience. Cities risk becoming corridors of throughput, rather than environments of dwelling. The culture of serendipity suffers not just from lack of attention, but from infrastructural neglect. What is not routed to is not maintained. And what is not maintained ceases to be part of the lived city.

There is also an educational cost. When children grow up with constant navigational assistance, they are less likely to develop strong spatial reasoning and map-reading skills. They are less likely to understand geography as a system of relations, and more likely to treat space as a sequence of app-mediated events. This affects how they conceptualise independence, risk, and problem-solving. To learn to navigate without assistance is to build a kind of embodied intelligence—a tacit trust in one's ability to read terrain, to infer, to recover from mistakes. It is not merely about finding a destination. It is about learning that unfamiliarity is not a threat, but a domain in which knowledge can be made.

Consider also how our bodies behave differently under different modes of navigation. Walking a route from memory engages us physically and cognitively. We scan the environment, reference landmarks, adjust our pace. But when following a digital path, movement becomes procedural. Eyes flick from screen to ground; decisions are deferred until prompted. Even our posture changes—shoulders forward, head down, attention partially elsewhere. The body becomes less an exploratory instrument and more a delivery mechanism for instructions. This is a subtle but significant disconnection from the physicality of space. Over time, it adds up—not only in what we miss visually, but in how we embody place. Where we used to inhabit space, we now transit through it.

Some might argue that digital navigation frees up mental bandwidth for more important things. But this presumes that wayfinding is not itself important—that it is a low-level cognitive chore best outsourced. This view fails to account for the richness of situational awareness, the quiet satisfaction of orientation, the long-term benefits of place memory. It ignores the affective quality of place—that the meanings we assign to streets and corners often arise from the unplanned: a smell, a sound, an unexpected turn. These meanings are what allow us to feel rooted. In removing the conditions for surprise, we risk severing our ability to form attachment. And in doing so, we become less at home in the very environments we move through every day.

The shift from exploration to execution is not inevitable. It is the product of tools, habits, and assumptions—many of which can be rethought. We can choose to deviate. We can choose to navigate without assistance, at least some of the time. We can walk without destinations, just to see what emerges. These acts are not nostalgic or anti-technological. They are forms of resistance to the narrowing of experience. They are ways to reclaim perceptual agency in a world that increasingly packages space as service. To wander is to reject the idea that everything must be known in advance. It is to assert that presence is more than arrival—and that meaning often lies just off the route we were told to take.

Cities Without Serendipity

Cities were never designed to be efficient. They were born out of complexity, constraint, and collision. For centuries, urban life was characterised not by order, but by overlap—of people, paths, purposes. Markets spilled into streets. Alleyways led nowhere and everywhere. Corners became stages for impromptu theatre, protest, flirtation, or pause. And it was within this friction—between strangers, stimuli, and spatial unpredictability—that cities earned their reputation as sites of creativity, culture, and human dynamism. Today, however, that rough-edged vibrancy is being quietly displaced. The ideal city is no longer messy—it is optimised. Smart cities, driven by sensors, algorithms, and data-driven design, now promise to tame urban disorder. But in smoothing out the chaos, they risk smoothing out the humanity that made cities worth inhabiting in the first place.

The language of smart cities is dominated by efficiency: streamlined transport, frictionless services, predictive infrastructure. It sounds good—who wouldn't want reduced congestion, optimised waste collection, responsive lighting, and instant access to public amenities? Yet each of these improvements rests on a particular assumption: that unpredictability is a flaw to be engineered out. The irony is that what makes cities livable, memorable, and meaningful often lies in what cannot be predicted. The unplanned encounter. The wrong turn that leads to a new neighbourhood. The overlooked park that becomes a personal sanctuary. *Serendipity is not a side-effect of urban life—it is a feature.* And it is increasingly under threat.

Navigation apps play a central role in this shift. Tools like Google Maps and Citymapper frame the city as a functional grid: origin, route, destination. They replace the experience of moving through a city with the act of executing a plan. Users are gently steered away from wandering, nudged towards routes that prioritise speed, convenience, or commercial interest. Even search results are algorithmically curated—what's "nearby" is shaped by ad spend, previous behaviour, or platform biases. The result is a narrowing of possibility masquerading as expanded access. Instead of discovering a local café by chance, we are shown the top-rated chain; instead of stumbling into a gallery, we follow the reviews. *We are no longer navigating the city—we are navigating a platform's interpretation of it.*

This phenomenon extends beyond individual behaviour. Urban planners, city officials, and private developers now rely heavily on data harvested from mobile devices, transport systems, and digital infrastructure to shape urban policy. Heatmaps of movement, predictive modelling of footfall, and AI-driven zoning tools all contribute to a new kind of spatial design—one that prioritises what is legible to machines. What's measurable becomes manageable; what's manageable becomes valuable. But what's not measurable—lingering, loitering, gazing, meandering—fades from the equation. The emotional cartography of a city—the subtle interplay between memory, attention, and place—is replaced by quantifiable flows.

Consider how the architecture of public space is changing. Benches are designed to discourage lingering. Transit hubs prioritise throughput over pause. Mixed-use neighbourhoods, once teeming with contradictions and asymmetries, are being replaced by planned developments with uniform aesthetics and frictionless functionality. These spaces are easy to navigate, easy to model—but also easy to forget. The city becomes interchangeable: a branded convenience rather than a distinctive character. The loss here is not merely cultural, but cognitive. Cities have long functioned as external memory systems—repositories of stories, spatial cues, and social learning. When everything is homogenised and signposted, when no corner feels distinctive, our ability to form mental maps and place-based identities weakens. *We remember less when everything looks the same.*

There is also a moral dimension to this shift. Smart cities often promise inclusion, but their infrastructures are rarely neutral. Data-driven systems can amplify existing inequalities by reinforcing dominant patterns. Predictive policing disproportionately targets marginalised communities. Real-time transit maps often ignore informal transit networks relied upon by lower-income residents. Seamless payment systems exclude those without bank accounts. In seeking to eliminate friction, these systems often eliminate complexity—and with it, the needs of those who don't conform to the model. Urban order, in this context, becomes not a shared good but a selective imposition.

Serendipity, by contrast, is radically democratic. It is one of the few urban experiences that cannot be fully optimised, targeted, or monetised. It emerges from unstructured movement, from sensory openness, from the willingness to not know exactly where one is going. It allows for permeability across class, culture, and purpose. A retiree and a student may both find themselves waiting in the same bookshop alcove, striking up a conversation neither planned. A street performer may alter the course of someone's day, or life. These moments are not measured in analytics dashboards, but they are the fabric of city life. To design them out in favour of managed predictability is to impoverish the urban experience.

The aesthetic of smoothness—of sleek architecture, polished interfaces, and synchronised logistics—has seduced not only developers but users. We have become conditioned to expect the city to work like an app: responsive, logical, pleasing. Yet cities are not apps. They are historical organisms, layered with contradiction, inertia, and improvisation. Their messiness is not a bug but a source of resilience. When every function is planned, the city loses its capacity to surprise. And when we stop being surprised, we stop paying attention. The numbing effect of predictability is not merely cognitive—it is ethical. A city that no longer asks us to see, to notice, to respond, also no longer asks us to care.

To be clear, this is not an argument against technology or progress. Real-time information, accessibility enhancements, and intelligent infrastructure can be transformative. But they must be implemented with an awareness of what they displace. A city cannot be reduced to a control panel. Nor should its designers assume that efficiency equals equity, or that seamlessness equals satisfaction. Urban life thrives in the gaps: between schedules, between destinations, between expectations. These gaps are where people improvise, connect, and discover. If we want to preserve the soul of the city, we must preserve its unpredictability.

This requires a different kind of design ethos—one that embraces ambiguity, supports informal use, and resists total optimisation. It means building spaces that invite pause and possibility: benches that welcome lingerers, streets without fixed purposes, signage that encourages exploration rather than compliance. It means protecting zones of low surveillance, where people can move without being tracked or profiled. And it means resisting the impulse to over-map, over-measure, over-manage. The smart city does not need to become the scripted city. Technology can support exploration, rather than curtail it, if we prioritise pluralism over control.

In the end, what makes a city livable is not its ability to tell us where we are or how to get there—it is its ability to surprise us along the way. Serendipity is not nostalgic whimsy. It is a civic value. It fosters empathy, curiosity, and adaptability. And it cannot be coded into a user interface. As we continue to digitise urban experience, we would do well to remember this: a city worth living in is not one that always works, but one that occasionally leaves us lost, only to find something better than what we were looking for.

Attention in Transit

The moments between places used to belong to us. The liminal spaces—on buses, in train stations, walking city streets—once offered something rare in the architecture of daily life: a pause without obligation. In these intervals, the mind could drift, rehearse memory, observe strangers, or simply sit in the idle current of motion. These were not wasted moments; they were unscheduled fragments of interior life. Today, however, most of these margins have been repurposed. Transit time has become screen time. The mental wilderness once shaped by glance, thought, and physical orientation is now colonised by dopamine triggers, curated feeds, and the hypnotic flicker of a touchscreen. What appears to be gained in entertainment and efficiency is matched—if not exceeded—by a subtler loss in cognitive spaciousness, narrative coherence, and perceptual engagement with the world around us.

It is not merely that we *can* fill our attention during transit—it is that every available interface assumes we *should*. Where a silent train journey once invited a gaze out the window, now the ambient assumption is that productivity or distraction is the superior use of time. Entertainment is on demand, but introspection is not. Apps do not encourage stillness; their economies are predicated on interaction. Waiting, once a form of contemplative discipline, is increasingly seen as an experience that must be padded, upgraded, or made to disappear. As a result, the mind rarely settles into the idle, low-stimulation state that researchers associate with insight, autobiographical memory, and creative problem-solving. *By interrupting boredom, we interrupt the mental processes that rely on it.*

This shift is not accidental. Entire industries have designed for this repurposing of attention. App developers speak of "micromoments"—the brief intervals between tasks or movements—as opportunities for engagement. Social media platforms are optimised to capitalise on these slices of transit time, offering content that can be consumed in seconds and refreshed endlessly. Streaming services preload clips to anticipate buffering delays. Even news apps are redesigned for single-thumb navigation, engineered not for depth but for frictionless continuation. *The result is not simply a new media diet; it is a new metabolic rhythm for attention itself.*

Transit is no longer a neutral medium. Consider how smartphones have reoriented the spatial experience of walking. Rather than encountering the city directly, eyes remain fixed on screens, often mediated by music or podcasts. Sensory input is filtered, peripheral vision is reduced, and the subtle awareness of one's surroundings—of who is nearby, of what has changed, of where one is in relation to landmarks—is diminished. The world becomes background. This desaturation of experience has implications not only for memory and mood but for empathy. Studies in environmental psychology suggest that unstructured observation—watching people, trees, street scenes—can increase social awareness and emotional regulation. When we outsource those observational moments to algorithmic curation, *we engage less with the unpredictable, the unscripted, the real.*

The economic stakes of attention repurposing are not minor. Attention has become a traded asset, and transit time represents a rare vein of unclaimed user engagement. Public transport systems are increasingly outfitted with Wi-Fi not primarily as a civic good, but as an extension of the commercial attention ecosystem. Commuter behaviour is mined to optimise ads, app use, and spending patterns. The shift from shared stillness to individual distraction is not simply cultural—it is infrastructural. Even the design of transit vehicles reflects this logic: seats are equipped with device holders, headphone jacks, USB chargers. Comfort is equated with connectivity. Silence becomes suspect.

There is also a temporal recalibration at play. Commuting once served as a psychological buffer between home and work, public and private roles. In the absence of screens, this transition allowed for emotional decompression. Now, the boundaries between roles are less defined. Emails are answered before stepping off the platform. Messages are replied to mid-stride. Content consumed on the commute bleeds into the workday or family dinner. *What was once preparatory becomes perpetual.* We no longer arrive—we are always already halfway somewhere else.

This has subtle consequences for mental continuity. The mind requires transitions. Without them, there is a fragmentation of inner narrative. Psychiatrist Esther Sternberg describes how physical movement through space—particularly walking or transit—acts as a scaffold for emotional processing. In these moments, we integrate recent experiences, resolve contradictions, rehearse conversations. When those moments are filled with externally generated stimuli, *we fail to process ourselves.* Over time, this accumulation of unprocessed cognitive residue can lead to a diminished sense of coherence.

We remember less not because we lack capacity, but because we lack intervals.

Defenders of screen time might argue that it enables learning, connection, or entertainment otherwise unavailable. And there is truth in that. Transit has always been a site of reading, reflection, and even conversation. Yet the distinction lies in the quality and intentionality of use. Reading a novel on the train is not the same as swiping through headlines or cycling between four apps. One invites narrative immersion; the other trades in fragmented alerts. *It is not the presence of stimulation that is at issue—it is the absence of psychic breathing room.*

The erosion of directional effort is another casualty worth noting. Navigation, once an active task requiring orientation, memory, and inference, is now a passive function of digital guidance. The result is a loss not only in spatial cognition but in narrative agency. To move through space without participating in the act of wayfinding is to relinquish a kind of authorship. We are led, not navigating. We follow instructions, not intuition. And when attention is outsourced during transit, the relationship to place becomes more abstract—less about being *somewhere* than about being *en route.* Place loses its texture.

This trend intersects with broader questions of autonomy. If our default response to being alone in motion is to seek curated distraction, what happens to our tolerance for ambiguity, discomfort, or solitude? These capacities are not luxuries—they are fundamental to self-regulation, creativity, and moral reasoning. A society that cannot sit still cannot think deeply. A culture that abolishes boredom abolishes one of the last remaining spaces for spontaneous thought.

There are glimmers of resistance. Initiatives promoting "digital sabbaths" or mindfulness in transit are gaining modest traction. Some train networks have introduced quiet carriages to preserve space for reflection. Urban designers are exploring environments that encourage lingering without scrolling. But these remain exceptions. The dominant tide pulls toward more engagement, more screens, more data.

To reclaim attention in transit is not a call for nostalgia or Luddism. It is a recognition that *not all progress is additive.* Some of it is subtractive in disguise. Reintroducing intervals of unclaimed awareness—those moments when nothing is demanded, expected, or delivered—may be among the most radical acts of autonomy available to us. In these moments, the self is not selling, responding, or consuming. It is simply attending.

And attention, properly reclaimed, is more than a faculty. It is a form of presence. Transit, then, need not be a void to fill. It can be a threshold. A space not just between places, but between states of mind. If we are to remain thinkers rather than merely users, observers rather than reactors, we must guard these thresholds. Not with rules or guilt—but with awareness, choice, and care. The time in between was never empty. We only stopped noticing.

The Missing Skill of Wayfinding

Before the compass, before road signs, before coordinates and satellites, there was the human body—orienting itself in space through intuition, memory, observation, and narrative. Wayfinding is one of the oldest cognitive abilities our species developed, foundational to survival long before it became a metaphor for clarity or direction. It is not merely a tool of travel, but an embodied intelligence—a hybrid of memory, perception, and decision-making that is both physical and deeply cognitive. Today, it is slipping into obsolescence. Not because we no longer move through space, but because *something else now moves us through it.*

The disappearance of wayfinding is not marked by drama or warning. It fades in increments, replaced by tools that promise certainty and convenience. GPS does not simply replace the map—it replaces the act of mapping. With it, our spatial attention contracts. We are no longer required to build a mental model of a place or calibrate a route based on sensory input. We become recipients of instructions rather than creators of orientation. While this may appear as progress, it comes at a cost: *we are outsourcing one of the most evolutionarily rich skills the brain possesses.* Navigation is not a trivial function—it is an anchor for memory, a rehearsal of agency, a bridge between person and place.

The anthropologist Tim Ingold noted that for most of human history, orientation emerged not from above but from within. People knew where they were because they had walked it, touched it, embedded it in story. In traditional cultures, navigation was intimately bound to myth, song, and narrative. The Polynesian concept of *wayfinding*—from which this chapter draws its name—was a masterwork of embodied geography. Using wave patterns, stars, birds, and memory, navigators could cross thousands of miles of ocean without a single instrument. What they possessed was not data, but attunement. *To find one's way was not just to arrive—it was to engage deeply with the world en route.*

Contemporary navigation systems have replaced this engagement with optimisation. The goal is no longer orientation but efficiency. Apps offer the "fastest route," prioritising time saved over spatial knowledge gained. Even walking apps reduce urban space to frictionless transit. You follow the blue dot, not the contours of the environment. What's lost is not simply the skill of finding your way—it is the ability to *know where you are* in any fuller sense. The disconnection is so complete that many users emerge from a journey with no memory of the streets, landmarks, or cardinal directions they passed. They arrived, but did not travel.

Cognitive scientists have begun to quantify these losses. The hippocampus, a region of the brain central to spatial memory and learning, is activated during active wayfinding. When we build mental maps—what psychologists call "cognitive maps"—the hippocampus strengthens. But when we are guided passively, those regions are underutilised. Over time, this has measurable consequences. A 2017 study at University College London found that habitual GPS users showed less hippocampal activity during navigation tasks, suggesting a kind of atrophy-by-inactivity. *Like a muscle no longer exercised, our internal compass grows weaker.*

Yet the implications stretch beyond anatomy. Wayfinding is also a form of narrative construction. To move through space intentionally is to stitch together landmarks, decisions, and paths into a coherent story. It is no coincidence that memory itself is often spatially encoded—we "map out" thoughts, "landmark" key ideas, "navigate" problems. When we lose spatial orientation, we lose one of the brain's primary scaffolds for organising experience. This affects not only how we travel, but how we think. Spatial reasoning, after all, is deeply tied to problem-solving, imagination, and even moral judgement.

There are psychological dimensions, too. Wayfinding cultivates resilience. To be lost is uncomfortable. It demands self-regulation, curiosity, and adaptive thinking. But it is also formative. It teaches persistence, pattern recognition, and improvisation. Getting un-lost is a rehearsal of agency. When that possibility is precluded—when the path is always shown, the decision always made for us—we forego the emotional learning embedded in uncertainty. *A society that never gets lost loses more than direction—it loses a critical theatre of self-reliance.*

Part of the erosion of wayfinding stems from our changing relationship with place. The more environments are engineered for uniformity and legibility—from airports to malls to algorithmically designed cities—the less they invite or reward exploration. This is compounded by smart technologies, which personalise and pre-filter experience. What remains is navigable, yes, but also stripped of mystery. We know where we're going, but not what we're missing. In this context, the skill of orienting oneself—of attending to details, feeling the grain of a neighbourhood, noticing the shift in light or language—becomes increasingly rare. *We are present in location but absent in place.*

Some might argue that the decline of wayfinding is a small price for the gains of efficiency. But this assumes that orientation is merely logistical—a means to get from A to B. It is not. Orientation is an epistemological act. To know where you are is to position yourself not only in geography but in context: social, historical, emotional. Wayfinding is a practice of attunement—of tuning the self to the world. It sharpens observation, grounds memory, and renders the abstract concrete. Its disappearance impoverishes our connection to reality.

This shift has generational effects. Children raised with digital maps do not develop the same spatial reasoning as those who navigate physically. They are more dependent, less confident in unfamiliar terrain. The developmental psychologist David Uttal notes that early exposure to real-world navigation—drawing routes, using cardinal directions, experiencing detours—correlates with stronger cognitive flexibility and spatial intelligence later in life. *To rob children of wayfinding is to rob them of a cognitive inheritance that took our species millennia to refine.*

And yet, the skill is not irretrievable. Like any embodied practice, it can be restored with use. The invitation is simple: get lost. Not carelessly, but deliberately. Walk without a destination. Travel without constant tracking. Engage with the landscape, not the interface. Ask for directions. Build maps in your mind. Navigate by smell, light, architecture. Use landmarks as anchors and the sky as a guide. Remember what it is like to find your way *by finding it.*

Wayfinding, at its core, is an expression of agency. In reclaiming it, we resist the outsourcing of our faculties to systems indifferent to our growth. We reclaim not only the skill, but the confidence it cultivates—the embodied certainty that we can locate ourselves in the world, even when the path is unclear. That we do not always need to be shown. That we can remember how to see.

And perhaps that is the larger lesson embedded in this vanishing skill: that orientation is not merely about geography. It is about presence. The capacity to *be where we are*, and to know it. In a world that constantly nudges us elsewhere, this is no small feat. Wayfinding reminds us that the path is not only something to follow—it is something we construct. With each step, with each turn, we declare: *I am here. I know where I've been. I can find what's next.*

Chapter 4
Decisions by Algorithm

A decision rarely begins at the moment of choice. It begins much earlier—quietly, invisibly—when the field of options has already been shaped. Defaults have been set, filters applied, and the logic behind what we see determined by systems we did not design. Increasingly, that invisible scaffolding is built by algorithms, whose purpose is not simply to reflect our preferences but to steer them. This gentle outsourcing of judgement—so smooth, so frictionless we hardly notice—has become one of the most far-reaching social experiments in modern life. And it unfolds not in labs or research trials, but in the everyday spaces where our attention gathers: search bars, recommendation feeds, navigation screens, auto-play menus.

The power of algorithmic decision-making lies not in coercion but in subtlety. Few of us feel directed; we still experience the satisfaction of deciding. That, of course, is the genius of it. Algorithms do not remove choice; they reshape the terrain in which it occurs. Take something as ordinary as picking a place to eat. What once involved curiosity, wandering, and conversation—peering into cafés, asking friends, glancing at menus—now begins with a handful of taps. "Top-rated near me." "Trending." "You might also like." A list materialises. But this list, though presented as neutral, has already been sorted—by optimisation models, proximity metrics, user data, and behavioural predictions. The horizon of possibility narrows before we even begin. We no longer see the world; we see its filtered simulation.

This quiet architecture of influence is what behavioural economists call "choice architecture." In its original sense, the term referred to the way the framing of options can shape outcomes—a principle as old as the cafeteria layout or the pension sign-up form. Yet in the digital era, the architect has changed. Human designers have given way to self-adjusting systems that perpetually adapt interfaces to data profiles. The architecture itself now learns. This automation creates a strange paradox: our lives are surrounded by infinite options, but our actual range of decision shrinks.

The effects are cultural as much as cognitive. Spotify's algorithm offers a "Daily Mix"—and we listen. Netflix queues the next episode—and we watch. Amazon suggests a product—and we buy. None of these are isolated choices; they are recursive. The more we follow, the more the system learns to reinforce what we already like. Diversity collapses into preference loops. A kind of algorithmic monoculture emerges, disguised as personalisation. We lose the old art of seeking, the pleasure of stumbling upon something alien or unexpected. Taste becomes less an act of cultivation than a by-product of recommendation.

This marks a deeper shift—from curation to consumption. Taste, once an expression of discernment, now appears pre-digested. The psychological shift is subtle: when the playlist generates itself, when the next read appears unbidden, our preferences start to feel automatic, almost innate. What was once a practice of attention becomes a reflex of habit. Convenience, for all its charm, carries a hidden cost—it trains passivity. Each act of delegation weakens our capacity for deliberation, exploration, and refusal.

Algorithms, it must be said, do not simply *offer* choices; they *accelerate* them. Their logic is anticipatory, predictive, impatient. Think of the GPS app rerouting your drive without explanation. The map redraws itself; you turn, almost unconsciously. The route optimises. You follow. The act of choosing collapses into a gesture of compliance. Efficiency, once a virtue, replaces understanding. You could rebel—

switch off, take another path—but almost no one does. After all, it's faster this way.

And so the same pattern repeats. Search results curated by relevance scores, predictive text finishing your sentence, smart assistants dimming the lights—all designed to collapse the interval between intention and action. That interval, though inconvenient, is where awareness once lived. Algorithms exist to remove that pause. Deliberation becomes inefficiency; ambiguity, an error state. The fork in the road still exists, but we no longer see it.

What fades in this process is more than the pleasure of pondering. The ability to choose *well*—to weigh, compare, imagine—is a human skill, one honed by effort and reflection. Decisions teach us values: what we prioritise, what we reject, what we're willing to risk. When algorithms mediate those micro-judgements, the developmental texture of decision-making erodes. Gradually, identity itself—formed through acts of selection and refusal—becomes something thinner, more mechanical. We drift, comfortably, through choices made on our behalf.

This is not to condemn algorithms outright. They bring undeniable efficiency, and sometimes even fairness. They reduce cognitive load, widen access, simplify complexity. The problem arises when we mistake their assistance for neutrality. Every system embeds incentives: what it optimises, what it ignores, what outcomes it rewards. To hand over choice without interrogating those priorities is to surrender more than convenience—it is to yield moral and cognitive agency.

At its core, the question is simple but pressing: are we still deciding, or merely agreeing? And if the latter, what does that mean for our capacity to question automation itself—to resist, to hesitate, to doubt? The issue is not technological progress but psychological surrender. The danger lies in ceasing to notice the moment delegation turns into dependence.

To study algorithmic choice is to re-encounter a timeless tension: freedom versus friction. Friction, though bothersome, is the cradle of reflection. It slows thought enough for awareness to enter. The hesitation before a decision—those few seconds of weighing and wondering—is where the self gathers itself. Systems that eliminate such pauses promise ease, but in doing so, they erode a small but vital rehearsal of autonomy.

The discussion ahead traces this quiet evolution: how choices are shaped and shortened, how our sense of judgement is being quietly rewritten by design, and how reclaiming the act of choosing might yet restore a measure of authorship. In a culture that automates everything from playlists to opinions, perhaps the radical act is simply this—to pause before accepting, to remember that the decision was once ours to make.

Choice Architecture

The decisions we believe we make are increasingly the outcomes of designs we never see. The path to action—whether it leads to a dinner reservation, a news article, a playlist, or a romantic match—is rarely carved by our conscious intent alone. More often, it is sculpted by algorithms that have already sorted, ranked, filtered, and curated a universe of options into a narrow corridor of recommendations. This process, largely invisible and frictionless, is known as *choice architecture*—the structuring of environments in which decisions are made, with the power to influence not only what we choose, but also what we believe was available to us in the first place. While the term originated in behavioural economics to describe subtle nudges in decision-making environments, it has taken on new urgency in a digital ecosystem where nearly all our options come pre-sorted by machine learning systems trained on our past behaviours.

One of the defining characteristics of modern algorithmic systems is their ability to anticipate what we want before we consciously know we're looking for it. Open a food delivery app and you're not presented with a blank map of culinary possibility; you're shown "Top Picks for You," often within metres of your last location. Launch a streaming service, and you're not offered a list of all available films alphabetically; you're served a carousel of thumbnails optimised for emotional click-through. Even a search engine, that paragon of choice, does not offer unfiltered access to the web. The first few results on any query page shape not only what we see but what we believe is true or common knowledge. *We rarely choose from a total set of possibilities—we choose from a pre-structured menu we didn't build.*

This narrowing begins well before the moment of choice. In dating apps, for instance, profile visibility is algorithmically governed—swipe right enough times on brunettes with university degrees, and the app will respond in kind. You are not sifting through a neutral pool of people; you are participating in a feedback loop where your prior behaviour shapes your future options. The illusion of abundance belies a reality of filtering. Even in e-commerce, Amazon does not simply list all products that match your query; it organises them by relevance, a metric that blends popularity, past purchases, vendor advertising spend, and your unique history. The very frame of visibility is rigged toward probabilistic predictions of what you're most likely to buy—not necessarily what you would have found compelling had you started from a position of full awareness.

This is not inherently malicious. In complex information environments, we *need* filters. Cognitive overload is real, and humans aren't equipped to manually evaluate thousands of options in real time. In this respect, algorithmic choice architecture offers real utility: speed, relevance, and personalisation. But these benefits carry costs, many of which are not immediately visible to the user. The most significant among them is the quiet erosion of *decision literacy*—the ability to tolerate ambiguity, weigh competing priorities, and sit with uncertainty. The act of choosing has been cognitively offloaded, and with it, a vital part of our developmental and moral reasoning capacities.

What is most intellectually pressing is not that algorithms are optimising for our preferences, but that they are *shaping* them. If we are consistently exposed to one type of restaurant, song, product, or person, over time our sense of what we like adjusts accordingly. This process of *preference formation* has been observed in social psychology for decades; familiarity breeds affinity. But in algorithmic environments, the conditions for exposure are opaque. As the philosopher Ruha Benjamin warns, "When machines decide, the mechanisms of power disappear behind a veil of objectivity." A recommendation engine may seem neutral, but it is ultimately an expression of incentives—those of the company that built it, the advertisers funding it, and the datasets used to train it.

We may think we are merely selecting from options, but we are often selecting from *pre-decided pathways*—roads paved by predictive logic, revenue models, and behavioural targeting. This has downstream consequences not just for consumer choice, but for public opinion, cultural taste, and civic awareness. News aggregators, for instance, don't just reflect what's happening in the world; they influence what we think *matters*. Personalised feeds mean that the headline you see might never be seen by your neighbour. What appears to be a choice—of what to read, what to believe, what to care about—is increasingly a function of curated exposure.

This introduces a vital epistemic tension: *If you don't know what you're not seeing, how can you know what you're missing?* In classical liberal frameworks, choice is predicated on access to information and deliberation. But in the digital age, access is mediated and deliberation is short-circuited. Algorithms don't just cater to demand; they help construct it. By showing us only what is most "relevant," they limit our cognitive periphery—the zone where new ideas, unexpected alternatives, and transformative encounters often live. In narrowing our inputs, they narrow our imaginations.

Moreover, the uniformity of algorithmic systems across platforms leads to a phenomenon sociologist Zeynep Tufekci calls *personalisation without personhood.* That is, although our digital experiences feel tailored, they are not the result of nuanced human understanding but of statistical modelling. Our choices become shaped less by idiosyncratic taste and more by clustering into user segments—demographic proxies designed to increase engagement and reduce unpredictability. This trend favours homogenisation. Users who share certain digital behaviours will increasingly be nudged toward similar content, which further collapses the range of exploration.

Choice architecture also plays out in how we navigate space. The routing algorithm in your GPS doesn't just find the fastest route—it decides which parts of your city you will *never see.* Regular reliance on optimisation tools means we bypass entire neighbourhoods, local shops, or lesser-known landmarks. These are not trivial omissions; they represent missed opportunities for connection, cultural exposure, and spontaneous learning. Optimisation flattens geography into transit efficiency, eroding our relationship with place and diminishing the micro-decisions that once animated daily life.

So what does autonomy look like under these conditions? It is no longer defined merely by the ability to choose, but by the *integrity of the environment in which those choices occur.* Do we have enough transparency to understand how options are being constructed for us? Do we possess the cognitive tools to question default paths? Are we aware of the criteria by which alternatives are excluded? Autonomy today requires not only personal freedom but *algorithmic literacy*—a fluency in recognising when our preferences are being manufactured and when our agency is being gently, invisibly re-routed.

The problem, then, is not that algorithms are involved in decision-making. The problem is that *we've forgotten they are*. Choice architecture in the digital age is marked by an unprecedented degree of behavioural predictability and psychological leverage. And while this can yield convenience and relevance, it also obscures the foundational principle of meaningful choice: that we are consciously engaged in the act of deciding.

To restore depth to our decisions, we must learn to interrogate the architecture itself. What is being optimised? What is being omitted? Who benefits from the recommended choice? These are not technical questions; they are civic, ethical, and existential ones. The future of freedom in a digitally mediated world may hinge less on the breadth of options and more on the *authenticity* of access—our ability to trace the origin of the menu from which we choose.

The Delegation of Taste

Curation was once an act of self-expression. What we read, watched, listened to, wore, and ate was a reflection not just of what was available, but of who we aspired to be. Taste, in this sense, was both personal and aspirational—a composite of exposure, effort, and identity. But in an ecosystem increasingly governed by algorithmic suggestion, the effortful practice of taste-making is giving way to the passive experience of being served. When autoplay queues our next video, when Spotify pre-loads a playlist tailored to our recent moods, when Amazon nudges us with "customers also bought," something essential is being offloaded: *our authorship of preference*. The delegation of taste is not merely a shift in convenience; it is a redefinition of cultural agency.

To understand the gravity of this shift, consider how often we now consume without actively choosing. You open Netflix intending to browse, but a trailer begins playing. The interface is engineered to reduce friction, to minimise pause, to anticipate. The same logic governs YouTube's autoplay, TikTok's infinite scroll, and Spotify's Discover Weekly. What begins as a personalised feed morphs quickly into a behavioural loop. Instead of searching for something specific, we lean back and *receive* whatever comes next. This is not curation—it is submission to a logic of relevance designed to maximise engagement rather than deepen discernment.

It is tempting to see this as harmless efficiency. After all, algorithmic curation often gets things "right": a song that fits your vibe, a book you hadn't heard of but now love, a show you didn't know you wanted. But the issue is not accuracy; it is *directionality*. Are we shaping our tastes, or are they being shaped for us? When recommendations precede intention, discovery becomes path-dependent. What we "like" becomes a feedback loop built on previous behaviours—some of which were not intentional to begin with. You clicked on a video out of boredom, lingered just long enough to signal interest, and now you're rewarded with more of the same. Over time, this recursive structure narrows exposure, calcifies habits, and builds cultural silos. *Taste becomes a mirror, not a window.*

The philosopher Pierre Bourdieu famously argued that taste is never neutral; it encodes social position, cultural capital, and economic power. In the digital age, that encoding has become automated. Recommendation engines are not designed to expand your palette; they are optimised to keep you watching, buying, or scrolling. What appears to be personalised is often a repackaging of the familiar. Diversity of experience is deprioritised in favour of predictability. The subtle result is that the architecture of cultural exposure is increasingly *convergent*, not exploratory. When everyone listens to the same trending songs, buys the same viral gadgets, or watches the same algorithmically promoted shows, we are not just delegating taste—we are participating in a mass homogenisation of culture under the guise of personalisation.

This is particularly evident in the aesthetics of platforms like Instagram and TikTok, where visual trends repeat with astonishing speed. The interior design you saw last week becomes the default template for a hundred others; the viral sound becomes the soundtrack of your feed for days. What feels like spontaneous taste formation is often the product of *platform amplification*. The algorithms favour certain content structures—quick cuts, bold colours, catchy hooks—and creators adjust accordingly. The result is an optimisation not just of consumption, but of production. Creators shape content to please the algorithm; consumers absorb content already shaped. Originality struggles to compete with reinforcement.

Yet the danger is not merely aesthetic conformity—it is the erosion of intentionality. Taste, when it functions well, requires tension. We gravitate toward what challenges us, moves us, even unsettles us. But challenge is rarely frictionless, and algorithms are trained to eliminate friction. They privilege the instantly appealing over the slow-burning. A difficult book, a dissonant album, an unfamiliar cuisine—all may be algorithmically invisible if they do not align with prior patterns. The cost of convenience is often *cultural atrophy*. We stop asking, "What might I come to appreciate?" and settle for "What do I already like?"

Moreover, when curation becomes invisible, so too does its ideology. Recommendation systems are not neutral mechanisms; they are commercial tools. Amazon's "customers also bought" is not merely informative—it is a subtle form of social proof engineered to accelerate sales. The playlists that auto-populate your music app are often shaped by industry partnerships, artist promotion deals, and monetisation strategies. Even social media platforms adjust visibility based on what keeps users engaged—not what might inform, educate, or broaden their view. In each case, the curation of experience is entangled with the logic of extraction. *We are not choosing in a vacuum—we are being chosen for.*

There are, of course, counter-arguments. One might say that algorithmic recommendations democratise taste—giving people access to things they would never have discovered on their own. There is truth in that. A teenager in Nairobi can discover Korean indie music, a retiree in Manchester can develop a taste for Japanese fiction. Exposure, once gatekept by geography or capital, is now algorithmically enabled. But the paradox is that these discoveries are often *bounded* by what the system is already willing to surface. The tail end of culture—the niche, the obscure, the unsponsored—is increasingly difficult to access unless you know exactly what you're looking for. And even then, search engines prioritise popular results. *What we find is increasingly what the system wants us to find.*

This delegation also affects how we understand our own preferences. When taste is no longer something we construct but something we consume, our sense of cultural authorship fades. We may enjoy a song but not know the artist. We may binge a series but never reflect on why it resonated. The experience becomes ambient, passive. Without the friction of decision, we lose the memory of deliberation. *And without deliberation, taste becomes less a marker of identity and more a trace of engagement history.*

The implications for education, politics, and civic life are profound. When readers are algorithmically funnelled into predictable news sources, when students rely on autocomplete for research, when citizens encounter only opinions that reflect their own, we are not merely consuming—we are being shaped. Taste, in these domains, becomes the infrastructure of worldview. And the more we outsource that infrastructure, the less we inhabit the practice of discernment.

What, then, might it mean to reclaim curation in an age of algorithmic recommendation? It is not about rejecting all digital tools; it is about *reinstating choice as a practice*. This could mean intentionally browsing beyond the first page of search results. It could mean subscribing to newsletters curated by humans, not bots. It could mean seeking out unfamiliar genres, following creators who challenge your assumptions, or reading books outside your algorithmic comfort zone. These acts are small, but they are gestures of agency. They reintroduce resistance into a system designed for ease. And in that resistance, taste becomes not just a by-product of behaviour, but a deliberate act of becoming.

Ultimately, taste is a form of commitment—an investment of time, attention, and values. To delegate it entirely is to surrender part of what makes us culturally distinct, intellectually alive, and aesthetically awake. The playlist may know what we like, but it cannot know what we *might* have liked had we given ourselves the chance to choose differently. The invitation, then, is not to reject technology, but to *reassert intentionality* within it. Because the algorithms will always keep serving. The question is whether we are still showing up to the table as authors of appetite—or merely its consumers.

The Disappearing Fork-in-the-Road

Modern life is increasingly navigated not through decisions but through defaults. Where once we paused to weigh, compare, and choose, we now glide through pre-sorted paths optimised by algorithms whose logic we rarely see and almost never question. The fork in the road—a space of deliberation, friction, and reflection—is being algorithmically flattened. What used to be a moment of consideration is now a moment of compliance, and the cost is not simply cognitive; it is existential. *We are outsourcing the experience of choosing itself.*

Consider Waze, the navigation app designed to shave seconds off your commute. It reroutes you automatically, often mid-drive, away from traffic or temporary obstructions. The convenience is undeniable. But so too is the subtle displacement of agency. There is no moment in which you stop and think, "Shall I go left or right here?" The decision is made for you in advance and enforced by a blinking blue line. This is not assistance; it is *substitution*. What's lost is the practice of navigation as a form of situated judgment. You are no longer engaged with your environment as a dynamic landscape requiring attention, estimation, or instinct. You are simply following instructions. And that shift—from deliberation to obedience—extends far beyond driving.

E-commerce has undergone a similar transformation. Shopping used to be a comparative process, a sequence of decisions shaped by curiosity, budget, aesthetics, need. Today, filters, recommendation engines, and predictive search structures frontload the experience. Before you even type, autofill anticipates. Before you scroll, "customers also viewed" has already narrowed the field. The interface suggests what people like you tend to prefer. It is not that choice has been removed—it's that *you've been nudged away from having to construct it yourself.* The fork in the road—Do I need this or that? Should I browse or explore?—has been replaced by a digital concierge who whispers, "Others like you chose this. Shall I order it for you?"

This architecture of pre-selection is often praised for its efficiency. It reduces overwhelm, speeds decision-making, and alleviates choice paralysis. But the very sensation of paralysis is itself a modern construction. It emerged in a culture where the volume of options exploded, and we lacked tools to sift through them meaningfully. Instead of teaching discernment, we engineered automation. The system didn't empower us to choose more wisely—it simply offered to choose *for* us. That tradeoff may feel benign, even helpful. But over time, it reshapes what it means to exercise agency.

Agency depends on the existence of *alternatives* that are visible, plausible, and reachable. In many algorithmically mediated spaces, those alternatives still exist—but we are no longer exposed to them. Consider smart home systems. Default thermostat settings, lighting preferences, morning routines—all programmable, all "intelligent." You can override them, of course. But how often do you? Once a pattern is set, it becomes the new normal. Why? Because convenience has a gravitational pull. It makes deviation feel like disruption. When defaults anticipate our needs, the decision to question them becomes not just unnecessary, but *inconvenient*. The result is a creeping habituation to the path of least resistance, where we stop even noticing that a fork ever existed.

One of the overlooked consequences of this design is the erosion of reflective pause. There is a kind of knowing that arises only in moments of indecision—when we are forced to articulate our preferences, to encounter our own ambiguity, to hold two options in tension. The fork in the road is not just a logistical problem; it is a psychological mirror. We see ourselves more clearly in the act of choosing. When that act is removed, so too is the opportunity for self-reflection. We move faster, but we know ourselves less.

This is not simply a philosophical issue. It has practical implications for competence, resilience, and adaptability. When decisions are constantly made on our behalf, we lose the habit of decision-making itself. Cognitive offloading, once a tool, becomes a crutch. The skills required to discern, compare, and prioritise atrophy through disuse. What began as a convenience becomes a constraint. You don't know what to cook without a recipe app. You don't know where to go without a navigation prompt. You don't know how to plan your day without your calendar notifications. *And you don't notice any of this until the system breaks.*

Contrast this with earlier forms of decision-making, which were embedded in context, story, and trial. A traveller once read landscapes—sun, wind, animal tracks, road signs—making sense of them through cumulative intuition. A shopper once remembered prices, compared brands, tried alternatives. A homeowner once adjusted routines through feedback loops of lived experience. These weren't always efficient systems, but they were experiential ones. They required presence, evaluation, adaptation. They embedded knowledge in action. The move from manual to predictive has not simply shifted the burden—it has shifted the *nature* of knowing.

Even more subtly, predictive technologies alter our sense of temporality. They collapse the space between impulse and outcome. You think it; the system acts. The delay that once allowed for reconsideration is gone. A rerouted trip is already recalculated. A product is one-click ordered. A playlist continues automatically. These are not trivial efficiencies—they are *structural compressions* of time, designed to reduce the micro-hesitations where doubt, preference, or deviation might emerge. And it is precisely in those hesitations that human intentionality lives.

The problem is not that predictive systems make decisions. It is that they *pre-empt* decision-making—removing the moment before the choice, the space in which reflection or re-direction might occur. This is what makes them epistemologically powerful. They shape not only what we do but what we *notice ourselves doing*. And if we don't see the fork in the road, we don't know we missed it.

Critics may argue that such concerns are overly nostalgic—that modern life is simply too complex for unassisted choice, that optimisation is rational, and that predictive tech frees us to focus on higher-order decisions. There is partial truth here. Not all decisions merit prolonged deliberation. But the question is not whether we should automate *some* decisions. The question is *which* ones, *why*, and *at what cumulative cost*. If every friction is designed away, then so too are the conditions for intentionality. And without intentionality, autonomy becomes aesthetic rather than functional—a posture we strike rather than a practice we inhabit.

To reinstate the fork in the road is not to reject technology; it is to insist on *seeing where paths diverge*. It is to design interfaces that reveal alternatives rather than conceal them. It is to build in pauses—not merely as failsafes, but as sites of value. Perhaps a navigation app could occasionally ask: "Fastest or most scenic?" Perhaps a shopping platform could make room for intentional browsing rather than predictive funnels. Perhaps a smart home could prompt, "Do you still want this to happen automatically?" Such gestures do not eliminate convenience; they *interrogate it*. And in doing so, they remind us that efficiency is not the same as wisdom.

Ultimately, the disappearing fork-in-the-road is not about roads, routes, or recommendations—it is about the cognitive architecture of modern agency. When we no longer have to choose, we may no longer remember *how* to. And when we forget how, we forget who. Identity, after all, is not just what we believe—it is what we *choose*, repeatedly, across time, in the presence of alternatives. To live meaningfully is to stand at the fork, see it clearly, and sometimes, *choose the slower path—not because it was offered, but because we decided it mattered.*

From Agency to Acceptance

One of the great illusions of the algorithmic age is that we are still fully in control. We scroll, we swipe, we click—decisions, yes, in a mechanical sense—but they are increasingly shaped by systems designed to narrow the field before we even become aware a field existed. The algorithm suggests; we respond. The system predicts; we comply. It all feels voluntary, yet our sense of authorship is thinning. Not because we are incapable of choosing, but because the *architecture of our choices* is being outsourced—and with it, the psychological muscle of agency begins to atrophy.

This shift is subtle but foundational. Agency—the sense that we are the originators of our decisions—is not just a matter of free will. It is a learned, practised capacity. To choose well, one must first notice that there *is* a choice, then evaluate options, tolerate uncertainty, commit, and take responsibility for the outcome. Each step demands effort and reflection. But modern systems of assistance are engineered to remove these very frictions. They aim to reduce doubt, accelerate selection, and increase satisfaction—often by eliminating the very conditions under which agency thrives.

Consider how streaming services like Netflix or Spotify present media. Autoplay, algorithmically sequenced playlists, and tailored "for you" content mean the next experience begins before a conscious choice is made. The decision-space is collapsed, not by force but by anticipatory design. The user is nudged into passive consumption under the guise of personalisation. Over time, the habit of actively selecting weakens. What was once a deliberate act becomes a seamless drift into whatever is cued next. *The user's competence in self-directed discovery diminishes, replaced by comfort with delegation.*

This is not a trivial evolution in interface design; it is a quiet reconfiguration of the self. Cognitive scientists have long understood that the brain reinforces what it repeatedly practises. As decisions are continually offloaded, the neural scaffolding that supports decision-making becomes less robust. Skills like discernment, weighing trade-offs, and reconciling conflicting values don't just vanish, but without active use, they degrade. The algorithm doesn't need to coerce us—it only needs to make choosing slightly harder than accepting. *Over time, that slight tilt becomes a behavioural slope.*

The psychological ramifications are evident in emerging patterns of decision fatigue and emotional outsourcing. People increasingly report feeling paralysed when forced to make unaided choices, even in low-stakes domains—what to cook, what book to read, where to travel. They defer to rankings, reviews, "most popular" labels, and trending tags. This deference is not merely informational; it becomes identity-forming. We come to see ourselves not as curators of experience but as efficient consumers of what's presented. *Our preferences begin to echo the system's offerings, and the line between what we want and what's available starts to blur.*

This feedback loop is especially visible in the context of smart home technology. From thermostats that learn your habits to fridges that restock themselves, the home becomes less a space of manual control and more an ecosystem of invisible algorithms. At first, it feels like liberation—why should we waste time adjusting the lights or remembering to reorder soap? But the deeper cost is psychological. When the home adapts without instruction, *we lose awareness of how our own rhythms are being shaped.* The routine is no longer authored but observed, and eventually, absorbed.

Importantly, the erosion of agency is not only a personal issue—it has social and political consequences. In democracies, agency underpins civic responsibility. It is the mechanism through which we interpret information, question authority, and act in accordance with principle rather than impulse. When our cognitive habits are sculpted toward passivity, our public selves follow suit. A society habituated to accepting suggestions over asserting judgment is one that becomes easier to manipulate—through feeds, filters, and frictionless persuasion.

There is also a profound shift in how identity is constructed. In a culture of algorithmic assistance, we no longer ask, "Who do I want to become?" but "What's next in the queue?" The arc of selfhood flattens into a series of system-driven prompts. Spotify learns your taste. Amazon tracks your purchases. Instagram shapes your aesthetics. You are reflected back to yourself through predictive patterns. But this mirroring is not neutral—it is a loop. The more you conform to what the algorithm expects, the more it reinforces that expectation. Novelty fades. Self-discovery becomes boxed into behavioural reinforcement. *You are what the system says you are—because that's what you keep clicking on.*

Yet this shift is not irreversible. The very plasticity of the brain that allows for habit erosion also allows for reactivation. But awareness is the first step. We must begin to *notice* when delegation becomes default, when convenience starts to mask compliance. That moment—when we sense that we've stopped choosing and started accepting—is the inflection point where agency can be reclaimed.

We see examples of resistance emerging in countercultural practices: digital minimalism, slow living, manual curation, even the return to analogue tools like notebooks, maps, or vinyl records. These aren't just nostalgic gestures—they are acts of *agency reclamation*. They say: "I want to choose with friction. I want to experience the cost of attention. I want to shape my environment, not just be shaped by it." Such movements remind us that competence is not innate but cultivated. That discernment grows not from being served, but from struggling to decide.

Still, any meaningful change must begin with a redefinition of what we consider "good" design. For decades, frictionless experience has been the holy grail of product development. But friction, in moderation, is not a flaw—it is a feature. It is where attention re-enters. A well-placed pause, an option to override, a prompt that says, "Are you sure?"—these can act as circuit-breakers in the flow of passive acceptance. They give the user back a moment of authorship. They make space for intention to breathe.

Designers, technologists, educators, and policymakers must begin to ask not just *how well* systems perform, but *what they train us to become*. Systems that remove too much effort also remove too much growth. There is no skill without struggle, no competence without practice. Agency, like muscle, must be exercised or it will wither. And what's at stake is not only how we navigate platforms, but how we navigate our own lives.

The next frontier is not merely personalisation, but *participation*. Systems must be designed not just to serve, but to involve—to surface options, to welcome interruption, to invite conscious rejection. This is not a call to abandon algorithms, but to *co-author* with them. To move from passive acceptance to active stewardship. To say, "I see what you suggest—but I choose otherwise." That simple defiance, practised consistently, is the groundwork of agency.

Ultimately, the difference between a life lived by algorithm and a life lived with autonomy is not always dramatic. It is often invisible. But it accumulates. In every choice made or bypassed, we are becoming someone. The question is whether we are becoming someone we intended—or simply someone *who happened to go along with the feed*.

Chapter 5
The Discomfort of Friction

Comfort has become the defining virtue of our digital era. Across nearly every sphere of life—from commuting to cooking, from correspondence to cognition—we have embraced systems that promise seamlessness, speed, and ease. Tasks that once demanded our full attention now unfold quietly in the background. Autocomplete finishes our sentences; navigation apps plot our courses; smart assistants manage playlists, appointments, and reminders. Even conversation itself is increasingly scaffolded by predictive prompts. And yet, beneath this engineered fluidity, an uncomfortable question lurks: what do we sacrifice when nothing is hard anymore?

To understand this drive toward frictionlessness, we must first acknowledge an evolutionary reality: the human brain is wired to conserve energy. Effort consumes resources—glucose, attention, focus—and, for our ancestors, economising energy was vital for survival. Avoiding unnecessary exertion made sense in the context of threats and scarcity. Yet in the contemporary landscape, where survival is rarely measured in calories conserved or steps spared, this same neural inclination can become a liability. Technology amplifies our innate preference for ease, quietly flattening the very conditions that cultivate growth, resilience, and character.

The irony is stark. Effort was once inseparable from understanding. Navigating physical terrain, for example, was more than following directions—it was an embodied exercise in mapping, memory, and spatial reasoning. Writing by hand or on typewriters embedded ideas in the mind differently than tapping a keyboard or dictating to a device. The friction of the process shaped cognition itself. Now, in a culture obsessed with optimisation, effort is often framed as inefficiency. Why write when you can dictate? Why remember when you can search? Why practise when you can automate?

This pursuit of ease, hailed as progress, masks a subtle erosion of faculties. By removing the small daily frictions of composing a message, solving a problem, or recalling a fact, we outsource the very processes that strengthen intellectual and emotional dexterity. Just as unused muscles atrophy, so too do neglected cognitive skills. What begins as convenience gradually becomes dependency. Over time, our tools do not serve us—they substitute for us.

The effects are most visible in language. Autocorrect, predictive text, templated responses: all reduce effort, yes, but also diminish intentionality. Tone, nuance, and meaning are flattened into pre-digested fragments. Smart replies in email, context-agnostic and brief, simulate engagement but remove the exercise of thought. We select rather than compose. This may appear trivial, yet it reflects a broader pattern: meaning is increasingly consumed rather than created.

Language, after all, is a vessel for identity. To articulate thought is to clarify the self. When communication tools diminish the need to work through what we mean, the feedback loop between thought and expression weakens. The friction once necessary for self-reflection and refinement is excised, leaving a subtle flattening of perspective and voice.

Navigation offers an equally revealing case. Previously, moving through a city or country demanded embodied orientation: memorising landmarks, noting spatial relationships, developing a sense of direction. GPS systems, with their constant recalibration, remove the need for any of this. Drift off-course and the system corrects itself. The brain disengages. Repeated studies link habitual GPS use with reduced hippocampal activity—the very centre of memory and wayfinding. In eliminating effort, we forfeit not only skill but the neural scaffolding that underpins exploration and spatial agency.

The consequences extend beyond neurons—they are cultural. A society trained to avoid difficulty develops an intolerance for ambiguity. Delays, disruptions, or unexpected challenges are framed as inefficiencies to be engineered away. In doing so, we forfeit the virtues cultivated by friction: patience, perseverance, adaptability. Consider cooking a meal from scratch versus ordering it through an app. The latter is efficient; the former instructive, teaching sequencing, timing, and care. By modern design standards, it is "inefficient." Yet inefficiency, properly understood, is often where depth and meaning reside.

The broader problem lies in what we now prize. Efficiency has become the measure of success—not merely in business, but in life. The path of least resistance is equated with the best path. But this metric blinds us to an essential truth: some of the most meaningful human endeavours are inefficient by design. Writing a book, nurturing a child, cultivating trust, mourning a loss—these cannot be sped through. They demand time, repeated failure, and sustained presence. When efficiency dominates, human experience flattens into a series of solvable tasks.

Addressing this imbalance requires more than nostalgia. It requires rethinking friction as a feature rather than a flaw. Constructive difficulty—effort that sharpens cognition, deepens emotional texture, and reinforces memory—must be recognised and preserved. This is not a rejection of technology, but a call for judicious use: knowing when automation serves, and when it supplants; when spellcheck aids creativity, and when it hinders it; when autofill streamlines form completion, and when it circumvents reflection.

Signs of a countercurrent are emerging. Educators reintroduce handwriting, not for sentimentality, but because it strengthens neural pathways more effectively than typing. Writers and artists return to analogue methods, not from technophobia, but to reconnect with the slowness that nurtures originality. Even technology design itself sometimes embraces "deliberate friction": two-step verification, "Are you sure?" prompts, delayed send functions—all pause the user, restoring responsibility and awareness.

The task is not to eliminate ease, but to discern where its ubiquity diminishes agency. When we never need to remember, we lose memory. When we never need to write, we lose voice. When we never need to orient ourselves, we become dependent. Friction, in its productive form, trains resilience. It makes thought robust. The question is not whether difficulty is inconvenient—it is—but whether it is worth it. In countless cases, it is.

This chapter confronts our cultural flight from difficulty not to lament the past, but to reclaim a fundamental dimension of human capacity. It offers a framework for recognising when efficiency has overreached and how to reintegrate forms of effort that build rather than erode. In a world increasingly defaulting to the automatic, we must ask: what do we become when we stop taking the hard route? The answer shapes not our productivity, but the very essence of who we are choosing to become.

Why We Avoid Difficulty

At a fundamental level, the human brain is a conservationist. It is designed not to maximise insight or mastery, but to minimise effort. The prefrontal cortex, responsible for complex reasoning and problem-solving, consumes a disproportionate amount of metabolic energy. Every time we choose the harder path—solving a novel problem, resisting an impulse, interpreting ambiguity—we engage a machinery that is metabolically expensive and evolutionarily cautious. This bias toward cognitive ease is not a character flaw; it is a survival adaptation. But when combined with modern technologies that pre-empt, automate, and simplify nearly every friction point of daily life, *what was once an evolutionary advantage becomes a liability to growth, attention, and agency.*

The contemporary digital ecosystem is architected around this neurological predilection. Every swipe, scroll, tap, and ping is optimised to be as low-resistance as possible. Interfaces are designed to reduce cognitive load, anticipating decisions before we consciously form them. Autoplay ensures that entertainment continues without our input. Shopping platforms sort and filter options to eliminate comparison work. Navigation apps remove the burden of spatial awareness. Even curiosity—one of our most valuable cognitive instincts—has been reframed through algorithmic suggestions, feeding us related content before we have the chance to form independent questions. In the name of usability, we have built systems that do our thinking for us, and the cost is rarely visible in the moment it's incurred. *But over time, the price is cognitive atrophy.*

Consider the example of learning. Decades of cognitive science have demonstrated what every teacher intuitively knows: *learning requires effort.* The phenomenon known as "desirable difficulty," first articulated by psychologists Robert and Elizabeth Bjork, describes how introducing manageable challenges—such as testing, interleaving, or spacing information—actually improves long-term retention. Struggle is not a bug in the learning process; it is a feature. Yet most educational technologies are not designed to preserve this productive tension. Instead, they are designed to smooth it out—by simplifying tasks, providing hints too early, or bypassing challenge altogether. In doing so, they reinforce the very bias we ought to be resisting: the notion that ease equals effectiveness.

This neurological inclination toward cognitive fluency—our preference for tasks that feel easy, fast, and familiar—is easily misinterpreted as intelligence. When a problem feels hard, we assume we are failing. When it feels easy, we assume we are succeeding. But this intuition is often inverted. Cognitive ease is associated with shallow processing and short-term recall. Cognitive difficulty, when carefully calibrated, leads to deeper encoding and conceptual integration. The discomfort of thinking deeply, then, is not a sign that we are out of our depth. It is often the signal that we are exactly where growth begins.

Modern design, however, privileges short-term satisfaction over long-term development. This is not limited to learning. In social interaction, the rise of predictive text and templated responses undermines the creative tension of articulating thoughts independently. In navigation, the elimination of disorientation removes opportunities for exploration and memory formation. In consumer behaviour, frictionless recommendation engines replace the internal labour of preference formation. *Each of these represents a micro-decision in favour of ease—and cumulatively, they represent a macro-shift away from autonomy.*

The psychology of this avoidance runs deeper than laziness. It is rooted in *affect*. Difficult tasks are not just metabolically demanding; they often feel emotionally uncomfortable. Uncertainty, ambiguity, and complexity trigger the amygdala, the brain's threat detection system. We seek to escape this discomfort—not because we are incapable, but because we are wired to interpret it as danger. Technology, in this sense, functions as a pacifier: it intercepts discomfort before we have the opportunity to reinterpret it as productive. And yet, *it is precisely in this discomfort that resilience, insight, and mastery are forged.*

Contrast this with the world of craftsmanship. A potter does not avoid the wheel because it resists the hand. A composer does not reject the score because it defies the first hearing.

These practitioners understand that *friction is formative*. It is the crucible through which fluency is earned, not circumvented. In intellectual life, the equivalent is deep reading, sustained writing, and problem-solving without shortcuts—acts that require attentional stamina and a tolerance for complexity. These capacities are increasingly endangered not by illiteracy, but by interface design.

In behavioural economics, the concept of "effort discounting" helps explain why we routinely devalue tasks that require more mental work, even when their outcomes are more rewarding. We are prone to select paths that demand the least immediate exertion, often at the expense of future competence. When this tendency is systemically enabled by our tools—when we are not only permitted but encouraged to avoid difficulty—we enter what might be called a *cognitive monoculture*. Everything feels easy, and therefore everything begins to feel the same. Originality declines. Problem-solving narrows. Even emotional range is compressed.

The cultural consequences of this are not trivial. A society that optimises exclusively for ease will eventually lose its appetite for challenge. Public discourse suffers, as people avoid complexity in favour of slogan. Art stagnates, as creators favour virality over vulnerability. Education plateaus, as students equate speed with mastery. In this climate, *the capacity to engage difficulty becomes a minority trait rather than a shared value*. And those who retain it—through deliberate practice, upbringing, or necessity—possess an increasingly rare form of cognitive strength.

To resist this trend requires intentionality. Not technological abstinence, but *technological discernment*. We must learn to recognise when ease is a gift and when it is a trap. When automation liberates attention, and when it displaces agency. When friction is wasteful, and when it is wisdom. This discernment cannot be programmed; it must be cultivated. It requires an awareness of our biases, a literacy in design, and a willingness to feel uncomfortable long enough to grow. It means choosing to read the book instead of the summary, to compose the sentence instead of selecting the suggestion, to struggle with the concept rather than Googling the answer.

To be clear, friction is not inherently virtuous. Poorly designed systems that create needless difficulty do not build character—they waste it. But *difficulty that is instructive, formative, or identity-shaping must not be eliminated on principle.* The challenge, then, is to design and inhabit environments that distinguish between the two. This is a design challenge not only for engineers, but for educators, leaders, and individuals. It asks: What kind of minds are our systems shaping? What kind of people do we become when every task is made effortless?

There are no easy answers—nor should there be. The value of this inquiry lies in its resistance to premature closure. It invites us to observe ourselves more clearly, to design our tools more responsibly, and to embrace friction as a resource rather than an error. To live without difficulty is to live without growth. And in a world increasingly engineered for ease, *our willingness to choose the harder path may be the most radical act of agency we have left.*

The Wisdom in Effort

Effort has been misbranded. In the prevailing cultural script, it is a sign of inefficiency, an obstacle to be engineered out. Why write by hand when you can type? Why type when you can dictate? Why search when an algorithm can predict? Yet this line of thinking overlooks a crucial paradox: that what effort demands, it also develops. *Friction is not merely a tax on productivity—it is a teacher, a trainer, and a form of investment in human depth.* The very processes we are designing away may be the very ones through which memory is strengthened, identity is forged, and moral clarity is earned.

One need only look at the act of handwriting to see this principle in action. Neurological studies have repeatedly demonstrated that writing by hand activates more regions of the brain than typing. When we write manually, we engage the visual, motor, and cognitive systems simultaneously, forming stronger memory traces and enhancing comprehension. The spatial arrangement of words, the muscle memory of letter formation, the temporal pacing of thought—these embodied elements of friction all contribute to deeper processing. A typed list may be quicker to produce, but a handwritten note is more likely to be remembered. *The slower act creates the stronger imprint.*

More than a cognitive aid, effort is also a builder of agency. Consider the experience of solving a difficult problem without shortcuts. Whether it is a mathematical proof, a legal argument, or a piece of code, the struggle to resolve ambiguity or contradiction does something structurally important to the mind: it strengthens pattern recognition, clarifies reasoning processes, and bolsters intellectual confidence. Each time we endure uncertainty without outsourcing it, we refine our capacity to act with autonomy. This is not a romantic defence of hardship, but a practical account of how *competence accrues through active resistance, not passive reception.*

Technology does not always erode these mechanisms—indeed, it can enhance them when used deliberately. But most modern systems are not built to amplify human capacity through challenge. They are optimised to remove it. Spell-check anticipates error before it occurs. Navigation apps render orientation obsolete. Recommendation engines collapse the world of possibilities into a narrow corridor of predictability. In each case, the friction that might have provoked attention, reflection, or self-correction is eliminated. What remains is speed, convenience, and—over time—a subtle flattening of cognitive texture.

Even our moral capacities, often assumed to be independent of interface design, are shaped by friction. Ethical decision-making is not a matter of fixed values alone; it is also a matter of deliberation. The ability to pause, to consider competing claims, to revise one's course—these are all forms of *moral muscle*, developed in situations that resist immediate clarity. The friction of opposing perspectives, complex trade-offs, or uncomfortable truths is not pleasant, but it is essential. Automation, by minimising these moments of tension, risks producing not only less thoughtful decisions, but *less thoughtful deciders.*

Physical navigation offers a tangible analogue. Before the ubiquity of GPS, moving through space required active participation. We read maps, constructed mental models, asked for directions, and made choices in real time. Getting lost was not simply an inconvenience—it was a crucible of attention, memory, and resilience. Wayfinding built not only spatial knowledge but *a sense of self-efficacy rooted in experience.* Today, a passive blue dot floats across a screen, demanding neither awareness nor recall. The skill remains latent, but the stimulus to engage it has vanished.

The shift from friction to fluidity is not merely technological—it is philosophical. It reflects a broader cultural belief that speed is inherently superior to slowness, that convenience is inherently superior to confrontation, that outputs matter more than the processes that produce them. But such beliefs are context-dependent, and increasingly maladaptive. In domains where human judgment, originality, or moral clarity are required, *the absence of friction may not be a sign of progress but of degradation.*

Indeed, many of history's most durable innovations emerged from deliberate difficulty. The scientific method, for instance, institutionalised friction—hypothesis, falsification, peer review—as a way of resisting premature closure. Literature, philosophy, and legal reasoning are disciplines defined not by their speed, but by their capacity to dwell in complexity. Education systems that produce long-term thinkers do not shield students from difficulty; they structure it, support it, and *treat it as an apprenticeship in autonomy.*

This is not a call for inefficiency for its own sake. There are domains—emergency medicine, disaster response, logistics—where reducing friction is not only beneficial but vital. But it is equally important to recognise where friction serves a developmental purpose. The key question is not whether a task can be automated, but *what is lost when it is.*

A culture that preserves the value of effort is not necessarily slower or less innovative. On the contrary, it is more resilient, more discerning, and better equipped to handle novelty. Such a culture does not fetishise struggle, but *understands it as formative.* It rewards those who persist through complexity, not just those who optimise for throughput. It teaches people to value the internal growth that comes from doing the hard thing, not simply the external result.

We might think of friction as a kind of ritual—an intentional slowing down that imbues an action with weight. Writing a condolence note by hand rather than sending a template message. Cooking a meal from scratch rather than ordering it. Preparing a lecture instead of relying on slides. These acts are not just expressive; they are formative. They change not only what we do but *who we become in the doing.*

In psychological terms, this is the difference between extrinsic and intrinsic effort. The former is effort expended in pursuit of an external reward—grades, promotions, likes. The latter is effort that is its own justification, valued for the integrity it builds. Systems designed to eliminate effort at every turn crowd out the possibility of intrinsic motivation. Over time, they produce users rather than learners, consumers rather than citizens, operators rather than creators.

This erosion is subtle, cumulative, and difficult to reverse. Once friction is eliminated, the skills it once fostered begin to atrophy. Worse still, the baseline expectation shifts. What was once considered normal effort becomes intolerable. What was once a fulfilling challenge becomes a frustrating obstacle. And the appetite for easy, instant, and automated only grows.

Yet it is possible to reintroduce effort in meaningful ways—not as punishment, but as a practice. Choosing to write longhand when clarity matters. Engaging in discussions that resist consensus. Walking instead of driving when orientation is needed. Each of these decisions may seem small, but *their cumulative impact is developmental.* They train us to remain present, to think clearly, to act with care.

Ultimately, the wisdom in effort is not an abstract ideal—it is a practical philosophy. It invites us to reframe difficulty not as damage to be avoided, but as *a form of investment in ourselves and others.* It asks us to recognise that what takes time also tends to leave a trace. And it challenges us to design lives—not just technologies—that make space for this trace to matter.

Automation and Erosion

The promise of automation has always been framed as liberation—from drudgery, error, inefficiency. We delegate tasks to machines not simply because they can perform them faster, but because they ostensibly perform them better. Yet as our devices complete more and more of our cognitive and social labour—correcting our spelling, composing our emails, even predicting our replies—the deeper question is not what automation adds, but *what it subtracts.* And increasingly, what it subtracts is skill. Not skill in the abstract, but embodied, practiced, context-aware human competencies—those fragile but essential capabilities that wither in disuse and erode when consistently bypassed.

Consider the common act of writing. Where once spelling, grammar, and sentence construction were part of a learned cognitive process, they are now backgrounded, auto-corrected in real time. Spell-check, predictive text, and grammar tools transform composition into a form of selection rather than generation. This may seem a trivial gain in efficiency, but the cognitive costs accumulate quietly. *The more we outsource fundamental linguistic functions, the less we retain the underlying proficiency to perform them unaided.* Over time, what was once skill becomes dependency, and dependency ossifies into unfamiliarity.

The effects are not limited to mechanics. Automation changes not only *how* we write, but *how we think while writing*. The friction of searching for the right word, the self-editing that accompanies re-reading, the structural thinking required to construct complex sentences—these all contribute to deeper articulation of thought. Remove the effort, and you risk removing the clarity. A machine may offer the perfect sentence, but the user has learned nothing about sentence construction. Worse, they may come to distrust their own voice, preferring the smoothness of the generated over the authenticity of the imperfect. *Skill atrophies not only through neglect, but through deference.*

This erosion extends into domains that depend not on language but on judgment. Auto-fill, for instance, saves time when completing repetitive forms. Yet it also disincentivises attention. A subtle shift in a form's context or legal implication may go unnoticed when fields are populated by default. Similarly, smart replies in email platforms reduce social interaction to pre-packaged scripts. They enable speed, but at the cost of nuance. Overuse of these tools trains users to skim rather than engage, to respond with efficiency rather than intention. *Politeness, empathy, humour—traits embedded in language—are flattened into transactional minimalism.*

There is a cognitive feedback loop at play. Tasks that once required small but repeated mental exertions now unfold with little awareness. Each time we bypass a minor challenge—recalling a password, phrasing a message, doing mental arithmetic—we avoid a moment of activation that, cumulatively, sustains mental fitness. The erosion is not dramatic but incremental, less like a sudden loss and more like the quiet dulling of a blade unused. We notice it not as an event, but as a fading: the fading of confidence in spelling without assistance, the fading of patience to articulate a complex idea, the fading of memory for tasks we once performed automatically.

Some might argue this is a fair trade. If machines can do it faster and better, why not let them? But this logic holds only if the goal is output alone. If the process itself is formative—if effort produces not just results but growth—then the calculus changes. *To automate a task is not to delete it, but to displace it—from human hands to digital scripts.* And when enough displacement occurs, a quiet cultural shift takes place: we begin to see effort itself as an inefficiency, rather than a source of depth.

One field where this tension is increasingly visible is education. Students trained in environments where spelling and grammar are auto-corrected, calculations are done by software, and writing is guided by templates may produce more polished assignments—but their underlying competencies are often shallower. Educators report declines in long-form reasoning, writing fluency, and even basic recall. This is not because students are less capable, but because their learning environment is structured to eliminate the very difficulties through which mastery develops. *The pedagogical erosion mirrors the technological one.*

The same is true in professional life. In domains such as law, journalism, engineering, or design, automation is now layered into every stage of production. And while these tools improve baseline efficiency, they also risk narrowing the practitioner's exposure to the full arc of their craft. A junior lawyer relying on precedent databases may never learn to structure an argument from first principles. A designer using AI-generated layouts may forgo the iterations that build aesthetic judgement. A journalist using templated leads may weaken their narrative instinct. *Skill becomes procedural rather than conceptual.*

This transformation is not inherently dystopian. Automation can support creativity, scaffold expertise, and free time for higher-order thinking—*but only when used consciously.* The problem is not that machines help us; it is that we forget *how* they help us, and what we lose when we forget the underlying skills they replace. Technologies that begin as tools often end as defaults, and defaults shape behaviour.

Social cognition, too, is subject to this erosion. Platforms that structure communication around templates and signals—likes, emojis, pre-set reactions—encourage compressed emotional expression. Interactions are faster, more frequent, but often less textured. The slow work of empathy—inferring tone, reading between lines, navigating ambiguity—is outsourced to interface cues. This affects not only how we relate to others, but how we develop relational capacities. As with language, *social fluency is learned through subtle, effortful encounters—not through automated responses.*

Perhaps the most insidious aspect of automation is that its erosion is often invisible. Because the interface is smooth, the process feels complete. Because the outcome is acceptable, the quality of the input is unquestioned. But over time, this illusion of competence can become dangerous. A person who has never written a formal letter, composed an argument, or navigated a complex conversation without assistance may struggle when the tool fails or the context changes. Resilience is built through variability, not constancy. *When we over-rely on automation, we become brittle—skilled at specific tasks in specific conditions, but underprepared for novelty.*

The answer is not to reject automation, but to re-evaluate its role. Where does it assist, and where does it replace? Which forms of friction are wasteful, and which are formative? What are we choosing when we choose convenience? These questions should not be rhetorical—they should inform design, policy, and personal practice. *Every automated task should prompt a second question: what skill does this task sustain, and do I still want that skill?*

Some efforts are worth preserving even if they are slower, less efficient, or harder. Not because difficulty is noble, but because difficulty often reveals what matters. The process of searching for a word, writing a thank-you note by hand, or solving a problem without assistance is not just nostalgic—it is neurologically and socially developmental. It affirms our place not as mere operators of systems, but as shapers of thought.

Automation is a tool; it is not a value. The erosion it produces is not inevitable, but it is insidious. Left unchecked, it recalibrates our thresholds for attention, intention, and complexity. But used wisely, it can also highlight what is worth retaining. And in that discernment lies our best hope—not to stop the march of automation, but to walk alongside it with clarity, care, and the unautomated discipline of choosing what to carry forward.

Rethinking Efficiency

It is a curiously modern reflex: when confronted with difficulty, delay, or ambiguity, we reach instinctively for efficiency. The logic is almost moral in tone—why waste time, why tolerate friction, why accept slow when fast is an option? Whether we are replying to emails, ordering groceries, navigating traffic, or planning our social lives, the default aspiration has become optimisation. Smooth interfaces, one-click purchases, predictive typing, batch processing—these are not merely conveniences, but expressions of a deeper assumption: that *faster is inherently better*. And yet, this foundational belief deserves interrogation. Because not all efficiency is benign. Sometimes, what we gain in speed, we lose in depth. And sometimes, the streamlined process becomes an anaesthetic—numbing us to the very texture of experience we once valued.

Efficiency is a powerful force because it speaks to both economics and psychology. It promises to maximise output while minimising input, to reduce errors, lower costs, and improve satisfaction. But its appeal is not just practical—it is existential. In a time-scarce culture, speed feels like control. To complete a task quickly is to assert mastery over time itself, to stay ahead of entropy. No wonder then that the pursuit of efficiency has colonised domains far beyond industrial production. We now apply it to communication, education, relationships, even moral decision-making. But *when every human activity is viewed through the lens of optimisation, something essential is displaced: the understanding that slowness, effort, and ambiguity are often not flaws in a system—but features of meaning itself.*

One of the first casualties of hyper-efficiency is autonomy. Consider the way we navigate cities. GPS apps like Waze or Google Maps don't simply assist—they prescribe. They offer one "best" route based on live traffic data, often accompanied by rerouting in real time. The driver becomes an executor of instructions, not an interpreter of context. The journey may be faster, but it is no longer exploratory. Local knowledge fades, directional memory weakens, and the subtle skill of situational navigation atrophies. What has been optimised away is not just the possibility of being lost, but also the possibility of *finding one's way*—a distinction with implications well beyond driving.

In the name of efficiency, we often forfeit deliberation. Algorithms now filter news, suggest entertainment, and rank search results—not by relevance to our long-term goals, but by predictive engagement. The outcome may be personalised, but the process is passive. We don't *choose* so much as we *confirm* what is served. What begins as time-saving becomes taste-shaping. *The speed of delivery conceals the narrowing of agency.* Over time, we forget how to sift, how to evaluate, how to be bored long enough to wonder what we actually want.

In education, the obsession with efficiency manifests in adaptive learning platforms, micro-credentialling, and skill-streaming apps that promise to deliver knowledge in digestible, high-yield formats. But the deepest forms of understanding are rarely efficient. They require grappling, reflection, repetition, and often the slow burn of confusion. A concept that takes minutes to explain can take weeks to integrate. Streamlining this process might raise test scores in the short term, but it risks hollowing out the learner's intellectual musculature. *To make learning frictionless is often to make it superficial.*

Even social interaction has been touched by the logic of efficiency. Smart replies, emoji reactions, and pre-loaded sentiment buttons compress communication into minimum viable emotion. They save time—but also flatten nuance. There is a qualitative difference between typing "Thank you" and tapping a thumbs-up icon. One conveys thought; the other, assent. At scale, these shortcuts shift the tone of human connection. Relationships that once deepened through shared struggle or awkward exchange are now conducted in smooth, curated bursts. *We mistake exchange for engagement.*

To question efficiency is not to endorse inefficiency for its own sake, but to ask: *what are we optimising for?* In a purely economic context, the answer is often clear—productivity, throughput, return on investment. But in human affairs, the goals are less quantifiable. What is the efficient path to wisdom? To trust? To moral clarity? These are not questions with simple metrics. In fact, the attempt to apply efficiency to such domains can be corrosive. A decision that is fast is not necessarily fair. A system that reduces emotional labour may also reduce empathy. *The values displaced by speed are often the ones we claim to cherish most.*

There are, of course, contexts in which efficiency is essential—emergency medicine, supply logistics, disaster response. But the danger lies in overextending this logic to situations where richness matters more than rapidity. For instance, when writing by hand, we slow the tempo of thought. This friction produces not just legible words, but legible cognition. When reading long-form prose, we absorb not only information, but cadence, tone, and structure—elements that resist skimming. When walking instead of driving, we encounter detail—the smell of a bakery, the weather's shift, a neighbour's greeting—that GPS cannot map. *What is lost in speed is not just data, but intimacy.*

A useful framework for evaluating the trade-offs of efficiency involves asking three simple questions:

What does this process prevent me from noticing? If automation or speed eliminates a point of contact with reality—a pause, a tactile interaction, a moment of ambiguity—then we must ask whether that loss impoverishes the experience. For instance, does relying on auto-fill prevent us from noticing patterns in our own information behaviours?

What competence is no longer required? Efficiency often involves the removal of human involvement. But if a process no longer demands skill, attention, or memory, what happens to those faculties? Are we saving effort, or surrendering capacity?

What kind of human am I becoming through this pattern? This is the most philosophical but also the most vital question.

Does this convenience reinforce a habit of avoidance? Does it cultivate dependency, passivity, or impatience? Does it align with the kind of presence, discipline, or character I want to develop?

The aim is not to reject efficiency wholesale. There is a place for speed, especially in repetitive or resource-intensive tasks. But *if we allow efficiency to dictate every domain of our lives, we risk becoming efficient in ways that make us smaller*. We become time-rich but meaning-poor, fast but shallow, productive but unformed.

The invitation, then, is not to slow down indiscriminately, but to discern *where slowness might be sacred*. To reclaim the moments where effort is not an error, but a teacher. To remember that not everything worth doing is worth doing quickly. And to recognise that the deepest forms of human intelligence—moral, creative, emotional—do not operate on the clock's terms.

Efficiency is a seductive promise, but also a fragile one. Its triumph depends on context. Its costs are cumulative. And its limits are rarely visible in real time. But if we look closely, we begin to see its shape—not as a virtue in itself, but as a tool whose value depends entirely on *what it serves*. And what we serve.

Chapter 6
Ambient Control

Step into a contemporary living space, and you may notice something curious: the room seems alive, anticipating your needs before you even articulate them. The thermostat adjusts as dusk falls, subtly responding not just to the hour but to patterns it has learned from you. Lights warm, dim, or brighten according to your prior preferences. Music shifts from morning upbeat to evening jazz with almost uncanny timing. This is not science fiction. It is the present reality of ambient control—systems quietly orchestrating our environment with minimal explicit input. Yet while these systems promise comfort, they also blur a crucial boundary: the line between control and surrender.

What distinguishes ambient control is its unobtrusiveness. Unlike older, more mechanical automation that demanded conscious operation, today's smart ecosystems observe micro-behaviours—raising blinds, dimming lights, skipping songs—and anticipate future needs. Convenience easily becomes choreography. But this choreography is not impartial. It is shaped by recommendation engines, proprietary algorithms, and predictive models aimed at maximising engagement or retention. The home becomes an interface; the body, a source of data. Our preferences shape the system, but over time, the system subtly shapes us in return.

The allure of ambient control is in its subtlety. The heat rises, the music changes, reminders ping at the perfect moment—and it feels as though these gestures are gifts: helpful, considerate, even personal. Yet the very helpfulness carries consequences. By shielding us from discomfort, randomness, and delay, these systems shield us from the experiences that cultivate resilience and adaptability. A thermostat that pre-empts energy use can dull awareness of temperature shifts. Lights that adapt to mood obscure natural variations in daylight. The more seamlessly the system "serves" us, the less we confront the raw conditions of reality.

Perhaps most consequential is the erosion of friction. Friction is formative: it teaches patience, tolerance for ambiguity, and a sense of cause and effect. Environments that constantly remove friction—from smart speakers finishing sentences to platforms anticipating purchases—interrupt this learning. We no longer wrestle with choices or settings; we accept the choreography. Cognitively, this diminishes agency. When effort becomes unnecessary, we are increasingly operating within preference loops we did not consciously author.

Feedback loops within smart environments illustrate this dynamic. Devices that learn from us simultaneously train us, nudging behaviour toward predictability. Play lo-fi music nightly at ten, and it becomes the default. Silence the phone at dinner twice, and notifications may be automatically suppressed. Micro-adjustments appear logical, even helpful, but they reinforce habitual patterns without conscious deliberation. Over time, we encounter an ambient inertia: a narrowing of variability that feels natural only because it is so subtly enforced.

Ambient control is unlike older technologies in its invisibility. There are no overt commands; the system observes, aggregates, and adjusts silently. Resistance is difficult—not because it is impossible, but because it often goes unnoticed. The most effective ambient intelligence is almost imperceptible. Yet this success comes with asymmetry. We are shaped more by the system than we shape it. Marketed as user-centric design, it often masquerades as autonomy while advancing system-centric convenience.

Early evidence suggests this over-optimisation has psychological consequences. Predictability may reduce stress in the short term but also diminishes novelty, serendipity, and cognitive stimulation. Minor surprises—forgotten favourite songs, unexpected breezes, unplanned conversations—become scarce. Ambient control, by design, privileges consistency over curiosity. Seamlessness may feel safe, but it risks dulling our engagement with the world.

There is an architectural dimension as well. Products increasingly exist as nodes in interconnected ecosystems: your phone links with your watch, your thermostat, your grocery list. Marketed as simplicity, this interdependence is also entanglement. Opting out demands disruption, relearning, inconvenience. The path of least resistance ensures users remain—not from loyalty, but from the friction of disconnection. It is a subtle strategy: dependence framed as ease.

Ambient control operates persuasively, not oppressively, aligning with human tendencies to conserve energy, avoid discomfort, and seek predictability. Yet support can evolve into substitution. Systems that manage environments may gradually displace our sense of stewardship, altering not only what we do but how we perceive our own agency.

Rejection of ambient intelligence is unnecessary. Its benefits are tangible. But living thoughtfully within such systems demands vigilance: noticing what is backgrounded, questioning defaults, and recognising how design shapes consciousness. We must ask not only, "Is this convenient?" but also, "What does this convenience cost—in attention, adaptability, or autonomy?"

This chapter examines these tensions: how smart systems personalise experience while eroding choice; how feedback loops optimise behaviour while fostering dependency; how seamlessness can masquerade as safety; and how environmental intelligence, if left unchecked, may diminish the capacities it purports to support. The aim is not resistance, but clarity. Ambient does not equal neutral, and intelligent environments—like intelligent people—require careful, conscious engagement.

Smart but Not Neutral

Walk into a modern home and you are no longer met by passive objects. You are entering a system of devices that listen, learn, and adapt. Lights brighten as you approach. The thermostat adjusts before you feel cold. Your voice triggers playlists, groceries, or ambient news. These conveniences feel intelligent—perhaps even intimate. But beneath their apparent helpfulness lies a profound asymmetry: *smart environments are not neutral terrains; they are selectively shaped by unseen logics, goals, and architectures of power.* Every adjustment that feels tailored may also be a nudge. Every automation may also be a decision outsourced.

The presumption of neutrality in technology is not new. We've long been encouraged to see tools as inert—means to ends, shaped only by user intent. But that framing collapses under scrutiny in today's ambient systems. Smart devices—ranging from thermostats and speakers to doorbells and kitchen appliances—are not just reactive, but predictive. They are driven by machine learning models that sort, anticipate, and often decide without input. These models do not emerge in a vacuum. They are trained on datasets that encode preferences, biases, and commercial priorities. *A smart device is only as neutral as the incentives of those who designed it.*

Consider the Amazon Echo, Google Nest, or Apple HomePod. Each is marketed as a personal assistant. Yet each also serves as a portal into a closed commercial ecosystem. Ask for a product recommendation, and the results are algorithmically filtered—not for objectivity, but profitability. Ask to play music, and your options are subtly prioritised by licensing agreements, engagement metrics, and platform strategy. These systems are not impartial librarians retrieving information. They are curators with vested interests, fine-tuned to maximise retention, consumption, and conversion. *To live in a smart home is often to live within a sales funnel disguised as support.*

Even when no product is being pushed, ambient control is shaped by implicit norms. Consider smart thermostats like Nest, which promise energy savings through behavioural learning. On the surface, this is benign: the system detects when you are home, learns your temperature preferences, and adjusts accordingly. But embedded within this is a value hierarchy—comfort is optimised against efficiency, and efficiency is defined not by the user but by algorithmic models of sustainability or cost-saving. You may never explicitly choose to reduce your carbon footprint, but the system nudges you toward it. Or it may decide that cost reduction matters more than personal comfort. *Control shifts not only from manual to automatic, but from conscious to opaque.*

The danger here is not in the presence of intelligence, but in its concealment. Smart systems rarely announce their logic. They do not explain their trade-offs. A smart assistant may skip certain results, never surfacing them. A smart fridge may suggest recipes based on past consumption without disclosing what was excluded. A robotic vacuum may map your floorplan and quietly transmit it to corporate servers—justified as a feature upgrade, never as a data collection protocol. In many cases, these behaviours are buried in terms of service or controlled through obscure settings few users alter. *Opacity is not a flaw; it is a design strategy that protects the system from scrutiny.*

The issue becomes sharper when personalisation intersects with surveillance. The data required to make a device "smart" is often behavioural—voice commands, location, routines, energy use, consumption patterns. That data, once captured, does not remain local. It is uploaded, processed, monetised. The smarter your environment, the more porous your privacy. And yet, because the feedback is immediate and helpful—your coffee machine knows your wake-up time, your light adjusts to your reading habits—*the erosion of privacy is framed as convenience.* What is lost is abstract; what is gained is tangible. Most users, understandably, never question the trade.

This subtle exchange—data for convenience, autonomy for automation—accumulates over time. The more the system adapts, the less the user intervenes. Over weeks and months, the interface disappears. Voice replaces touch. Recommendations replace decisions. Defaults replace deliberation. This is the hidden strength of ambient technology: it does not demand behaviour; it *absorbs* it. And through this absorption, it shapes what becomes normal. You stop questioning the playlist because it always plays what you like. You stop checking the temperature because it always feels fine. But *what you like and what feels fine are not fixed—they are the results of ongoing calibration between you and a system designed to influence you.*

One might ask: is this influence always negative? Certainly not. A thermostat that lowers heating during absence saves energy. A speaker that avoids disturbing neighbours may be considerate. A smart doorbell that flags unknown faces could deter intrusion. But even here, value-laden assumptions creep in. Who decides which faces are suspicious? Who defines optimal temperature? Who controls the thresholds for volume, light, or access? *Smart systems encode normative judgments, often without making those judgments visible.* And when those systems are mass-produced by global corporations, local nuance or individual needs are often subordinated to scale.

The issue is not that we are being manipulated in nefarious ways, but that we are being shaped by systems we do not fully see or question. The intelligence behind smart environments operates like infrastructure: once embedded, it fades into the background, becoming part of the expected world. And like all infrastructure, it channels behaviour. We adapt to its presence. *The very success of ambient intelligence lies in its invisibility.* And that is where the greatest danger resides—not in overt coercion, but in the quiet redefinition of norms through automated design.

What would it mean to live with smart technologies that are *intelligible* rather than just intelligent? Imagine devices that explained their decisions, offered alternatives, exposed their weighting criteria. Imagine systems designed for *user sovereignty* rather than just engagement. This is not a utopian fantasy. It is a matter of design philosophy. It is the difference between systems that see users as data sources and systems that see them as partners. *Transparency is not anti-innovation; it is the condition for trust.*

To understand that smart environments are not neutral is to open a space for critical engagement. It means asking not just *what* a device does, but *why* it does it, and *for whom*. It means noticing the subtle nudges, questioning the assumptions, tracing the lines of influence. And it means remembering that behind every "smart" decision is a set of human choices—about values, incentives, and goals—encoded into machines that now surround us. These choices deserve our attention, not just our compliance.

The future of ambient control does not hinge on smarter devices alone. It hinges on the quality of the relationships we forge with them. Those relationships will only be as ethical, empowering, and human as the design decisions that structure them. *Smart is not the same as good. Adaptive is not the same as fair. Helpful is not the same as neutral.* If we want agency within the systems that shape us, we must treat them not as magic, but as constructs—built by people, for purposes that must be made visible. Only then can we live not just inside ambient environments, but *with awareness* of them.

Invisible Feedback Loops

Every tap, pause, scroll, or click in a digital environment feeds a system that observes, interprets, and recalibrates in real time. These actions—seemingly inconsequential—form the substrate of vast algorithmic engines that learn not merely *what* we prefer, but *how* we behave. The promise of this machine learning architecture is personalisation: a more tailored, efficient, and "user-friendly" experience. But embedded within this promise is a recursive paradox—*as these systems learn from us, they also begin to shape what we do next.* We are no longer simply users of information technologies; we are participants in *feedback loops that train and are trained by the tools themselves.* And critically, we often do not know when we've crossed that line.

The defining feature of a feedback loop is its circularity. Output becomes input. In natural systems, such loops help maintain equilibrium—homeostasis in biology, self-regulation in ecosystems. In technological systems, however, especially those optimised for engagement, feedback can magnify rather than balance. Recommendation engines, for instance, surface content based on past behaviour: the videos we watch, the purchases we make, the songs we skip. But once presented, these recommendations *influence* subsequent behaviour. What we consume next becomes *less a choice and more a reaction.* The user is not merely selecting—they are being steered.

Netflix's autoplay is a canonical case. When one episode ends and the next begins within seconds, the system reduces the space for decision-making. The feedback loop tightens: watch, autoplay, watch again. Over time, data accumulates not just on what we *like,* but how long we persist, when we abandon a show, which genres keep us engaged past midnight. These metrics are fed into a model that updates itself constantly—not to broaden our horizons, but to maximise retention. The result is content engineered not just for quality or storytelling, but *for stickiness*. The loop becomes less about discovery, more about reinforcement.

Smart assistants like Alexa and Google Assistant operate similarly. They learn when you issue commands, how you phrase them, which routines you rely on. As their voice recognition sharpens, so too does their ability to anticipate. A thermostat suggests heating adjustments before you ask. A speaker proposes your morning news brief without prompt. Initially, this feels intelligent. But with repetition, *the system trains us to expect rather than initiate*. Behavioural autonomy is eroded not through force, but through convenience—until *the absence of a suggestion feels like friction*.

Even thermostats—devices once associated with fixed-function control—have become subtle behavioural engineers. Consider Google Nest. It observes when you're home, what temperatures you favour, when you adjust settings. From this data, it constructs a model that anticipates your comfort thresholds. But in doing so, it subtly redefines them. If the system infers that you tolerate 19°C in the evenings and adjusts accordingly, over time *you internalise that expectation*. What was once a deliberate preference becomes a default. The line between *what you want* and *what you've learned to accept* blurs.

What makes these feedback loops especially powerful is their *opacity*. Users rarely know the exact mechanisms by which recommendations are generated. The "because you watched..." tag on Netflix or "customers also bought..." on Amazon signals correlation, not logic. Few understand what features were weighted, what alternative options were excluded, or whether commercial incentives influenced the results. In theory, personalisation reflects you. In practice, it also reflects a platform's strategy—whether to promote exclusives, clear inventory, or amplify content that drives higher engagement metrics. *The feedback loop does not simply mirror your preferences; it curates them within constraints you cannot see.*

Over time, such loops can narrow the diversity of input. A music app that sees you listen to 90s rock may offer a near-infinite playlist in that genre—rarely surfacing jazz, ambient, or classical unless explicitly prompted. A news aggregator that sees you reading centre-left commentary may suppress centre-right perspectives, not as censorship, but as statistical optimisation. The longer the loop runs, the more homogeneous the feed. *Personalisation becomes insulation.* And insulation, though comfortable, breeds fragility. It limits exposure to new forms, ideas, and intellectual discomforts that might otherwise expand our cognitive range.

This phenomenon has been extensively studied in the context of social media. The term "filter bubble," popularised by Eli Pariser, captures the reinforcing logic of algorithmic curation. Facebook's news feed, Twitter's trending topics, TikTok's For You page—all are governed by algorithms that learn from engagement and serve more of the same. The loop intensifies around emotion: content that angers, excites, or provokes is more likely to drive interaction, and thus be promoted. But this skews perception. The world becomes not what it is, but what the loop thinks you will react to. And *your reactions, shaped by what you're shown, reinforce the loop's confidence in its model of you.*

This dynamic extends far beyond content. In e-commerce, Amazon's recommendation engine influences what products are visible, which ones climb rankings, which sellers succeed. In navigation, apps like Waze and Google Maps use collective user data to reroute traffic—but by doing so, they redistribute congestion, sometimes shifting it into vulnerable residential areas. In both cases, user input trains the system, but user behaviour is also *guided by it.* The system does not just respond; it orchestrates.

The implications for autonomy are profound. Feedback loops alter not only what choices we see, but *how we define choosing*. When every input feeds into a model that adjusts outputs, free will becomes entangled with prediction. We start behaving in ways the system expects because that is what the system presents as viable. Over time, preferences may ossify—not because we truly love what we're consuming, but because we've stopped encountering alternatives. *This is not coercion—it is habituation through algorithmic design*.

Yet the solution is not to abandon these systems. Personalisation, at its best, offers efficiency, relevance, and ease. The goal is not rejection, but critical clarity. We need to understand when a recommendation is helpful and when it is narrowing. We need interfaces that allow transparency—why was this suggested? What else could I have seen?—and give users the ability to adjust, override, or opt out of certain loops. *Agency is not about removing automation; it's about reintroducing intelligibility*.

Some platforms have begun offering tools for this. Spotify's "taste breakers" playlists encourage users to explore genres outside their usual patterns. YouTube allows clearing of watch history to reset the recommendation algorithm. But such tools are often buried, under-promoted, or poorly explained. *The loop, once formed, is not easily broken*. And even when it is, the user often pays the cost—in time, in effort, in friction.

The deeper challenge is cultural. In a world trained to expect immediacy, surprise and uncertainty are often experienced as inefficiency. But uncertainty is essential for growth, novelty, and serendipity. A healthy system must not only respond to our habits but occasionally *interrupt them*. It must include space for unpredictability, ambiguity, and contradiction. Only then can feedback loops evolve into feedback systems—not self-reinforcing spirals, but dynamic, open circuits that honour both memory and possibility.

Ultimately, invisible feedback loops reveal a deeper truth about the interface between humans and technology: *every intelligent system we build ends up building us in return*. What we consume shapes what we are offered. What we are offered shapes what we believe is possible. And what we believe is possible shapes how we live. If we want to remain authors of our behaviour—rather than the sum of our clickstreams—we must learn to see these loops not as conveniences, but as structures. They can guide us. But we must also learn to push back.

The Psychological Toll of Predictability

Comfort is not neutral. As digital systems continue to refine our environments for seamlessness, convenience, and minimal interruption, something subtler and more consequential begins to wane—our tolerance for uncertainty, our capacity for boredom, and our appetite for novelty. It is easy to assume that optimising for ease is a net positive, and in many domains it is. But what happens when the world begins to behave exactly as we expect it to? When recommendations never surprise, thermostats anticipate our warmth before we notice the chill, and calendar reminders eliminate the need to remember anything at all? *The paradox is that in designing for maximum control and predictability, we may be undermining the very psychological flexibility that allows us to thrive in a messy, uncertain world.*

The human brain evolved not for stasis, but for adaptation. Our cognitive architecture is wired for unpredictability: pattern detection, surprise evaluation, problem-solving under pressure. In evolutionary terms, *novelty signalled opportunity or danger*—requiring attention, triggering learning, prompting behavioural refinement. This is not an argument for chaos, but for calibrated disorder. When every variable is controlled, every environment pre-emptively managed, *the brain's engagement with the world becomes flatter, duller, and narrower.* In an ambiently controlled ecosystem, spontaneity becomes rare not because we no longer value it, but because the conditions for it have quietly eroded.

Consider the mundane magic of Spotify's algorithm. A user who once spent hours curating playlists now finds that the system creates a soundtrack based on past listening patterns. The music is often good—pleasant, attuned, inoffensive. But it also becomes background, predictable. The friction of discovery, once part of the listening experience, is now largely absent. *The user becomes a passive consumer of musical déjà vu.* This erosion of surprise may seem trivial, but it mirrors a broader cognitive shift: *we lose the micro-moments that force us to pay attention, to decide, to be curious.*

Smart homes operate on a similar principle. Lights adjust based on detected movement. Voice assistants queue reminders. Climate control systems respond to occupancy patterns. These efficiencies are genuinely useful. Yet the more a system pre-empts a user's needs, the less engaged that user becomes with their environment. *Ambient control dulls situational awareness.* When thermostats think for us, we no longer monitor how we feel. When doors lock themselves, we stop remembering whether we checked them. *Convenience displaces conscious action.* And as it does, the sense of being an active participant in one's space begins to dissolve.

Predictability also warps perception of time. In a world where everything arrives on demand—food, content, transportation—the moments between intention and fulfilment are compressed. Waiting becomes obsolete. But *those pauses once served as spaces for reflection, adjustment, recalibration.* When they are eliminated, the present becomes a continuous stream of expected outcomes. The unexpected is no longer exhilarating—it is jarring. It is not merely that people dislike surprises; it is that systems no longer allow for them. This contributes to what some psychologists term "temporal homogeneity"—a flattening of lived experience where days blur, novelty recedes, and memory formation weakens. Without unpredictability, *the brain has fewer anchor points from which to distinguish one moment from another.*

This is not a theoretical concern. Research into boredom, for example, has shown that it plays a critical role in creativity and self-regulation. Far from being an obstacle, boredom acts as a signal—it tells us that our current mode of engagement is insufficient, prompting a search for novelty or purpose. But in hyper-optimised environments, boredom is aggressively designed out. Algorithmic feeds ensure that every scroll presents something marginally interesting. Streaming platforms ensure that something is always playing. Notifications manufacture urgency. As a result, *we become less practiced in tolerating mental stillness, and less capable of acting autonomously when stimulation is withdrawn*.

There is also a social cost. Predictability undermines the interpersonal friction that builds resilience. In digital communication, for instance, smart replies—those brief, auto-generated email or messaging responses—remove the need to formulate one's own expression. While efficient, they flatten emotional nuance. When most interactions are mediated through optimised systems, there are fewer missteps, fewer negotiations, fewer unexpected conversations. *The serendipity of human contact is displaced by interactional templates.* Over time, users internalise these efficiencies, leading to a kind of conversational automation in which originality and depth decline. Communication becomes safer—but also thinner.

Even architectural spaces reflect this shift. Smart offices, for instance, adapt lighting, temperature, and soundscapes based on occupancy and preference. Employees are less distracted, more comfortable. Yet studies in environmental psychology suggest that variability—changes in texture, temperature, light—is key to sustained attention. *We focus better not because our surroundings are controlled, but because they are interesting.* Predictability, once again, undermines engagement by reducing sensory diversity. The physical environment becomes a backdrop rather than a participant in cognition.

One might argue that predictability is a privilege. And in many ways, it is. Not having to worry about safety, sustenance, or logistics is a product of technological and societal progress. But when predictability becomes the default mode of experience, we risk habituating to it in ways that lower our psychological resilience. In the face of ambiguity, those accustomed to certainty may experience disproportionate stress. *Over-optimised lives breed underprepared minds.*

This vulnerability is compounded by the fact that ambient control is often invisible. The user does not always realise how much has been pre-set, auto-regulated, or nudged on their behalf. Thermostats suggest settings without explanation. Feed algorithms decide relevance with opaque logic. Smart assistants adjust preferences silently. The experience is smooth—but smoothness conceals structure. *We confuse ease with neutrality.* But these systems are not neutral. They are governed by assumptions, parameters, and optimisations that may not align with the user's long-term wellbeing. And because these systems rarely ask for consent in the moment—only blanket agreement at setup—users are absorbed into a regime of control without awareness, let alone resistance.

A culture of hyper-efficiency leaves little room for mess. But messiness—interruptions, delays, wrong turns—is often where growth occurs. Spontaneity, by definition, cannot be preloaded. It requires margin: *unstructured time, ambiguous input, moments not yet assigned a function*. As systems grow better at shaping behaviour to predictability, those margins shrink. People become more efficient but less exploratory. More productive but less imaginative.

To counter this, designers and users alike must ask a difficult question: when does the pursuit of frictionlessness become a form of constraint? *Not all control is control over others; much of it is control over possibility*. We don't just lose spontaneity—we forget that it was ever an option. Reintroducing variability, then, is not a regression but a recalibration. It means designing systems that occasionally resist, challenge, or surprise. It means curating spaces—digital and physical—where ambiguity is allowed to breathe.

Ultimately, psychological flexibility depends not on total predictability, but on the capacity to navigate the unpredictable. Systems that remove all error, variation, or interruption may offer comfort in the short term, but they risk diminishing the deeper faculties that enable growth, adaptation, and meaning. *To live well is not to automate every discomfort; it is to discern which discomforts are worth keeping.* And in doing so, we begin to reclaim a cognitive environment rich in possibility—not simply one designed to be easy.

Designing for Dependence

Convenience is rarely free. It may not charge interest or require a password, but it exacts a subtler toll: *a slow erosion of self-reliance masked as progress*. What appears on the surface as user-centred design—intuitive interfaces, frictionless navigation, personalised assistance—often conceals a deeper structure: ecosystems engineered not simply to serve, but to habituate. The goal is no longer to help users perform a task, but to keep them inside a system where those tasks never need to be questioned, learned, or adapted independently again. The result is not just loyalty—it is *dependence*.

Consider the architecture of the smartphone. It is a portable command centre for life: messaging, banking, scheduling, entertainment, navigation, identification, photography. What once required a constellation of tools—maps, cash, keys, newspapers, alarm clocks—has been absorbed into a single device. The promise is power. But it is also captivity. Each function is delivered through closed ecosystems designed to prevent departure. Apple's iOS environment, for example, encourages users to stay within native apps: Safari over Chrome, iMessage over WhatsApp, Apple Pay over competitors. Google's ecosystem operates in parallel logic. These design choices are not accidental; they are *deliberate constraints that make independence feel inconvenient.* The more seamless the experience, the harder it becomes to imagine—or tolerate—alternatives.

This consolidation is not inherently sinister. Many users prefer the efficiency of integration. But what's often overlooked is that *ease of use quietly becomes inertia*. Once a user delegates their habits, memory, or social rituals to a convenience platform, extracting oneself becomes effortful. The system has become not just a tool, but a default. We stop noticing how it shapes our routines because it *is* the routine.

Amazon's ecosystem is an archetype of this logic. Prime membership is not simply a delivery service; it is a bundle of convenience cues: streaming, groceries, smart home integration, one-click purchasing. The effect is that Amazon becomes not a choice among options, but *the environment in which choices are made*. Even the idea of searching elsewhere becomes marginalised—why compare prices when Amazon's algorithms already anticipate your preferences? The friction to exit increases over time—not through any overt constraint, but because *the convenience is always one step ahead of resistance.*

This is where resilience begins to falter. When every step of the process is smoothed out—when groceries arrive with a tap, tasks are scheduled by AI, emails are drafted with autocomplete—the individual's ability to improvise, troubleshoot, or persist through friction diminishes. *The muscle of adaptability atrophies through disuse.* A person who has relied for years on GPS may no longer possess a mental map of their own city. A student raised on predictive typing may struggle to write fluently without prompts. A consumer accustomed to algorithmic recommendations may lose the curiosity to browse beyond the obvious. What looks like freedom from effort is often a silent trade: *autonomy for automation.*

To understand the full effect of this, we must examine how dependence is designed into the user experience. Every convenience system operates on behavioural feedback. The more data a user supplies—through clicks, pauses, purchases, corrections—the more tailored the system becomes. This loop increases perceived relevance, which in turn increases use, which generates more data, which refines the loop. It is not malevolent. But it is *sticky*. Unlike traditional tools, which require intentional engagement, digital ecosystems shape behaviour passively. *They reward repetition and familiarity over exploration and uncertainty.* The environment nudges users toward more of what they've already done.

This is visible in platforms like Netflix, where the autoplay function eliminates decision-making; or in Google Search, where autocomplete gently directs the shape of the question. These are not mere interface decisions—they are *behavioural constraints that redefine what users notice, consider, and choose.* Over time, such constraints scaffold dependence not only on content, but on the structure of interaction itself. *People don't just rely on the tool—they come to rely on the mode of thinking the tool encourages.*

One might ask: is dependence always bad? Is it not part of civilisation itself that we outsource certain capacities in exchange for others? Writing allowed memory to be externalised; cars replaced walking; calculators overtook arithmetic. But the crucial distinction lies in *what gets preserved alongside what gets offloaded.* Healthy delegation retains understanding. Designing for dependence, by contrast, *severs comprehension from use.* A person may drive every day without understanding how an engine works—but if the system breaks, they still understand how to navigate or ask for help. A system designed for dependence, however, prevents even that basic fallback. When it fails, *the user is stranded—unable to repair, reroute, or reimagine.*

This erosion of flexibility has significant consequences for adaptability. In environments where systems operate smoothly, users are rarely required to engage with underlying complexity. This makes sense when everything works. But complexity is inevitable. Software updates, infrastructure failures, economic shifts—these are not bugs but features of any large system. A person habituated to complete reliability may find such disruptions disproportionately disorienting. *Resilience is not a trait we inherit—it is a habit we practise.* And systems designed for dependence discourage that practice by solving problems before the user is even aware of them.

Education offers a revealing case study. Platforms like Grammarly or ChatGPT streamline writing, removing friction in grammar, syntax, structure, even tone. Students benefit from support. But there's a risk: when the platform guides the thinking as much as the writing, *the user learns to trust the system over their own judgement.* The danger is not that assistance exists—but that it becomes invisible, unexamined, assumed. Over time, the writer may cease to ask whether a sentence is clear, elegant, or persuasive; they ask only whether the system approves.

What, then, is the alternative? Designing for *complementarity* rather than dependence. This means building systems that assist without absorbing. Tools that support decision-making without pre-empting it. Interfaces that invite reflection, not just action. *A resilient user is one who can step outside the system without paralysis.* This does not mean rejecting convenience. It means *being intentional about which skills we wish to retain, and which we are willing to let recede.*

A simple example illustrates this balance. Consider a navigation app that not only gives turn-by-turn directions, but overlays a visible map, highlighting landmarks, alternate routes, and potential points of interest. Such a system supports the journey without obscuring it. The user remains situationally aware, capable of switching paths or recovering from error. *Assistance does not eclipse comprehension.* Compare this to a system that offers only an arrow and distance: perfectly efficient, but cognitively sterile. When the arrow disappears, so too does the sense of orientation.

Convenience is not inherently a trap. But it becomes one when its logic is totalising—when the system absorbs every step, every friction, every trace of deliberation. *Dependence is not just about what we cannot do—it is about what we no longer think to try.* When tools become extensions of infrastructure rather than extensions of thought, we begin to experience the world less as participants, and more as managed nodes within it.

The future of human agency depends on the choices made at the level of design. Systems can scaffold our abilities or supplant them. They can invite engagement or discourage it. They can remind us that we are capable of improvisation—or make us forget that improvisation was ever necessary. *The real cost of convenience is not time saved—it is capacity unpractised.* And in a world where volatility is the new normal, *unpractised capacity is risk.*

To reclaim adaptability, we must be more than users. We must be stewards of our own competencies, even as we benefit from the systems around us. This begins not with dramatic rejection, but with subtle shifts: turning off autocomplete, pausing before accepting a recommendation, navigating without GPS once in a while. These are not acts of rebellion. They are acts of *preservation*. In doing so, we remember what it feels like to be not just efficient, but *capable*—and to belong not just to systems, but to ourselves.

Chapter 7
Digital Mirrors

We once encountered ourselves in quiet, unhurried spaces—reflections in glass, notes in journals, or the steady gaze of those who knew us deeply. Today, that mirror has been largely replaced by screens. Our sense of self has become mediated, scrollable, and responsive to algorithms. Who we are—or at least how we think we are performing—is increasingly filtered through systems designed to measure, compare, and broadcast. Not with ill intent, but with precision. Every heartbeat logged, every meal tracked, every status shared renders identity dense with data yet strangely thin in context. What once emerged organically now arrives as output.

There is a pervasive assumption that visibility equates to truth. Fitness trackers promise insight into the body, social platforms promise connection, productivity apps quantify value in minutes saved or goals ticked off. Yet each tool carries an implicit bias: what is measured becomes important, and what is important is performed. Data ceases to be merely descriptive; it curates, structures, and ultimately constructs the self. A morning jog is incomplete until logged; a fleeting moment is unreal until posted. Internal validation has ceded ground to notification chimes.

The implications run deep. Self-tracking, initially heralded as empowering, increasingly drives anxiety, performativity, and the erosion of private meaning. When steps or hours slept are reduced to numbers, the body becomes a dashboard. When exercise must double as content, the act shifts from health to display. Gamification permeates intimate routines. Habits, once instruments of growth, now populate a public-facing narrative of self-improvement. Meditation streaks, sleep scores, learning badges—they motivate, but they also reshape the intention behind the activity. What begins as genuine can subtly drift into performative ritual; the reward can overshadow the experience itself.

This movement from intrinsic to extrinsic motivation is not accidental. Social platforms, quantified-self tools, and feedback-rich interfaces exploit behavioural loops: cue, action, reward. Designed to encourage engagement, these systems align neatly with dopamine pathways. Likes, retweets, rings on a smartwatch—they create feedback loops of recognition. In such an environment, the mind begins to optimise for applause. Measurable actions gain preference; preferred actions become habitual; habits crystallise into identity.

Metrics are often arbitrary, yet their influence is real. Consider a Fitbit user pacing to hit a step goal or a student completing an online badge for recognition rather than learning. These behaviours are not glitches; they are inherent to systems that privilege quantifiability over substance. A deeper question emerges: when we curate for visibility, who or what do we leave behind? Each performance sacrifices spontaneity, privacy, and the space for ambiguity. To live visibly is to live selectively.

At the heart of this shift lies the construction of selfhood itself. Pre-digital identity was narrated, built through memory, social interaction, and private reflection. It bore contradictions, rough edges, and pauses between perception and performance. The digital self, in contrast, often presents as continuous, polished, self-conscious. It is shaped not merely by what we share, but by anticipated affirmation. Over time, the public self risks eclipsing the private: a post that succeeds validates existence; one that fails quietly disappears, as though never lived.

Social media amplifies this compression, rendering identity into a series of high-resolution snapshots, each inviting feedback, each feeding algorithmic curation. Community becomes audience. The subtle pressure to remain legible—consistent in persona, aesthetic, or belief—discourages nuance and growth. The self becomes less a work in progress and more a curated product line.

Here the digital mirror warps reality. It reflects not who we are, but what systems value: engagement, exposure, optimisation. In pursuing these metrics, we internalise a paradox: connection increases, yet certainty about ourselves diminishes. The platform does not merely show—it instructs. Even private thought risks preconditioning by public possibility.

Critically engaging with this transformation does not require rejecting technology. Rather, it demands awareness. The questions are simple yet essential: when do tools intended for self-knowledge become instruments of self-distortion? Where lies the boundary between enhancement and dependence? Technologies that began as aids to reflection or motivation have, as they become ambient and essential, shifted from mirrors to scripts.

Framing identity as data also reshapes values. Emotional nuance, moral struggle, private failure—cannot be graphed. Yet these are the textures of growth. In a metrics-driven environment, the unmeasured is often devalued. The consequence is a flattening of personal complexity, a drift toward normative optimisation: fitter, happier, more productive—always visible, always improving. But a life constantly optimised may not be a life truly lived.

If selfhood relies on continuity through change, what occurs when change is calibrated by metrics designed by others? Who defines progress? Who sets goals? The digital mirror rarely answers these questions explicitly, yet they are embedded in the interface. Rejecting it outright would be Luddite; accepting it uncritically risks forfeiting authorship of the self.

This chapter interrogates the cost of that surrender. Its aim is not abstention but agency; not moralising, but illumination. Identity at its richest is dialogue, not dashboard. Without reclaiming the space and language for that dialogue, performance may be mistaken for personhood, feedback for fulfilment, attention for meaning. The digital mirror is not passive. It gazes back. And unless we meet that gaze with discernment, we risk existing as reflections: accurate, efficient, yet profoundly empty.

Selfhood in Metrics

A person checks their sleep quality before deciding how rested they feel. Another opens their phone to verify if they've walked enough steps to justify their dessert. A third contemplates whether the meditation session "counts" if it didn't extend their streak on an app. These are not anomalies—they are symptoms of a new ontological order, where identity is not simply lived but *logged*. Today, an increasing share of our behaviour is monitored, measured, and converted into data points. But the transformation is not one-way: the data doesn't just describe us—it *defines* us. Quietly, the act of quantification begins to rewire the architecture of the self.

What begins as tracking soon becomes framing. Activity monitors, diet apps, time-logging tools, social analytics dashboards—these were sold as aids to self-awareness, but their hidden influence runs deeper. In reducing complexity to countable units, they elevate the *measurable* and sideline the *meaningful*. We start by asking, "How am I doing?" but increasingly settle for "What does the data say?" And if the data says you're doing well—even if you feel hollow—you may dismiss the feeling. If it says you're underperforming—even when flourishing in other dimensions—you may feel behind. *Numbers, once neutral, acquire moral gravity*.

Nowhere is this shift more visible than in the "quantified self" movement. Initially popularised by technophiles seeking bio-optimisation, it has seeped into mainstream culture through fitness wearables, wellness dashboards, and even productivity analytics. Apple Watches buzz with reminders to stand, rings to close, and averages to beat. Strava turns casual jogs into leaderboard contests. Sleep apps assign nightly scores. The consequence? *We begin to relate to our bodies and minds not as integrated wholes, but as modular systems in need of continuous upgrade.* One's morning mood becomes a variable shaped by Fitbit metrics rather than inner cues. Over time, the authority of these numbers supersedes the wisdom of introspection.

This reorientation extends beyond the body. Social media platforms provide perhaps the most invasive metricisation of identity. Likes, comments, shares, follower counts—each serves as a proxy for approval, visibility, or relevance. But these proxies are deceptive. What garners attention is not necessarily what carries substance. The frictionless feedback loop subtly shifts content creation from expression to performance. Photos are edited, captions curated, timelines cleaned—all to conform to an algorithmic model of desirability. As a result, the *self presented becomes increasingly filtered*, and the self experienced becomes increasingly contingent.

Yet the psychological cost of such externalisation is not merely superficial. As metrics come to dominate feedback loops once filled by reflection, conversation, or personal resonance, intrinsic motivation erodes. When every behaviour can be scored, it becomes difficult to act without imagining the metric that might result. You no longer write for clarity or joy—you write for engagement. You don't read out of curiosity but to complete your Goodreads target. You don't walk to clear your head—you walk to hit 10,000 steps. *Behaviours shift from being internally meaningful to externally accountable.*

One might argue that quantification is merely a new mirror—an objective aid to self-understanding. But mirrors do not choose what to reflect. Metric systems do. They foreground some dimensions of human life while rendering others invisible. No app rewards you for patience, forgiveness, wonder, or intellectual humility. There is no dashboard for nuance. This bias toward the countable distorts how we prioritise our time, our goals, and even our moral orientation. *What cannot be measured begins to feel less real, and what is real becomes subordinate to what is trackable.*

Consider the act of journaling—a historically intimate and reflective practice. When digitised and gamified, even this becomes externalised. Apps like Daylio reduce lived complexity to mood emojis and activity checkboxes. A good day is a high-data day. But what happens to emotions that don't fit clean categories? Where do we put ambiguity, contradiction, the richness of unsorted thought? The tools that promise to help us know ourselves better may in fact teach us to bypass knowing altogether, replacing slow insight with fast statistics.

This is not to dismiss all metrics. Indeed, in fields like medicine, education, and logistics, quantification has revolutionised accuracy and accountability. But the danger lies in assuming that what works for systems can work identically for selves. The human psyche resists precision; it thrives in paradox. Reducing it to trendlines and averages is not neutral—it is an act of cultural authorship. And it raises urgent philosophical questions: *What happens to agency in a world of real-time analytics? What becomes of authenticity in a context that favours legibility over complexity?*

One consequence is that *identity becomes increasingly referential.* Rather than being a coherent thread woven through time, it becomes a mosaic of numerical updates. You are no longer just someone who writes—you are someone who published X posts, gained Y followers, received Z likes. You are not just a student—you are a dashboard of GPA, module completion, and app-generated study minutes. These units abstract away the experience and sediment instead a managerial view of the self. You don't feel *in* your life—you feel like you are monitoring it.

The problem is compounded by the commercial architecture surrounding most metrics. Behind every quantified-self platform is a business model. The app that tracks your sleep also sells subscriptions. The network that shows your post analytics also sells your data. *Metrics serve users, but they are also behavioural scaffolding for platform profits.* The more you track, the more you engage. The more you engage, the more you conform to the feedback structures embedded in the tool. And so, slowly, almost invisibly, your behaviour adapts—not to your own values, but to the architecture's imperatives.

There are counterarguments, of course. Some see these tools as modern rituals of self-mastery. Others point to how tracking can reveal harmful patterns, enable healthier habits, or facilitate collective goals. These are valid points. But the question is not whether metrics can help—it is *how they help*, and at what cost. The loss of unquantified space—the kind in which we make sense of ourselves without audience or analytics—may be one of the most profound cultural shifts of our time. *It is in such spaces that imagination, moral introspection, and long-form memory find room to grow.*

Without those spaces, selfhood risks becoming modular—composed of interchangeable data points rather than continuous narrative. The richness of being human, however, lies not in efficiency or even improvement but in complexity. In growth that isn't linear. In motives that resist explanation. In relationships that are valuable not because they're frequent, but because they're meaningful. A culture obsessed with metrics flattens this richness. It encourages self-alignment with what is rewarded—visible success, perpetual optimisation, quantifiable output—while marginalising the slow, the subtle, the non-transactional.

We must, then, ask not only *what* we measure, but *why*. And perhaps more importantly, *what we neglect* in the process. As philosopher Byung-Chul Han has argued, the quantified subject becomes transparent but also disposable. The more visible the self becomes, the more interchangeable it is. Uniqueness requires interiority—an inner space beyond metrics. If that space is crowded out by dashboards and graphs, we risk raising a generation fluent in performance and impoverished in reflection.

To navigate this terrain wisely, we must develop a new literacy—*a literacy of metrics and their meanings*. This involves knowing when data clarifies and when it distorts; when it enhances autonomy and when it undermines it. It means cultivating zones of resistance—practices that are deliberately untracked, moments that remain private, experiences that are their own justification. The goal is not rejection of technology but a restoration of perspective: *metrics are tools, not truths.*

The self is not a spreadsheet. It is a story. And while numbers can play a role in telling that story, they are not the story itself. If we forget this, we may gain legibility at the cost of substance, efficiency at the cost of depth, and validation at the cost of authenticity. In an age increasingly defined by metrics, the quiet act of reclaiming narrative may be one of the most human—and most urgent—forms of resistance.

Gamification of the Everyday

A digital confetti burst rewards you for brushing your teeth. A ring lights up on your watch when you complete your movement goal. A productivity app celebrates your fifth consecutive day of writing. These moments may feel trivial, but they are not without consequence. Gamification—the use of game-like rewards, visuals, and feedback mechanisms in non-game contexts—has colonised the mundane. It converts daily behaviours into achievement systems, not to make them meaningful, but to make them addictive. *In doing so, it reorients motivation: from inner purpose to outer reward, from intrinsic intention to extrinsic affirmation.*

Originally, gamification promised to enhance engagement and simplify complex tasks. It was an idea rooted in good faith: make healthy habits fun, foster consistency, inject delight into dry routines. But as the model matured, it revealed a more complex psychology. The badge, streak, or level-up is not a neutral nudge—it is an engine of behavioural design. It creates a currency of achievement that is legible to platforms, but not always meaningful to the person. What matters becomes what's rewarded. The visible, the trackable, the streak-worthy—these gain status, while subtler forms of value fade into neglect.

Consider Duolingo. The app has drawn tens of millions into daily language practice, using streaks, leaderboards, and cartoon characters to sustain interest. But many users confess that their loyalty shifts from learning to *maintaining the streak*. The motivation morphs: not fluency, not cultural literacy, but keeping a digital counter alive. When the streak breaks, the practice often collapses. *The gamified structure hijacks attention—first as tool, then as master.* And in this transition, motivation is externalised. You stop acting because it matters to you; you act because the system is watching.

This phenomenon extends far beyond education apps. Fitness platforms reward users for step counts, exercise minutes, or calorie burns—metrics that are, at best, proxies for health. But health is multifaceted. It includes rest, play, stillness, and social nourishment—qualities hard to count and harder to gamify. Yet once a metric is visible, it becomes dominant. A person may override their body's signals to meet their daily goal, redefining wellness as compliance with the app. *When behaviour is shaped by the logic of games, even well-being becomes a performance.*

The psychology underpinning gamification is Pavlovian. Variable rewards—rewards that arrive unpredictably—are known to be more compelling than predictable ones. This is the same principle that drives slot machines. Add to that elements of social comparison, such as public badges or shared leaderboards, and you have a potent recipe for compulsive behaviour. But unlike traditional games, which are entered voluntarily and ended at will, gamified environments bleed into everyday life. You don't just *play* the game—you *live* in it. The boundaries blur, and the rules are often invisible.

Motivation, long studied by psychologists as a delicate interplay of autonomy, competence, and relatedness, is not immune to these structural shifts. Gamification, especially when poorly designed, undermines autonomy by replacing volition with obligation. It flattens competence into scores. It distorts relatedness into competition. The result is not enhanced engagement, but a hollow mimicry of it—what sociologist Zygmunt Bauman might call *liquid commitment*: fast, shallow, endlessly repeatable, but never anchored. *People may show up, but they no longer know why.*

Even more insidious is how gamification normalises surveillance. To issue rewards, systems must first observe. Every input—every word typed, meal logged, step taken—is captured and analysed. The logic of gaming becomes the logic of tracking. This isn't always coercive, but it is cumulative. The reward scaffolding creates a quiet contract: participation in exchange for oversight. Over time, the very idea of self-regulation is replaced by app-delegated monitoring. *You no longer ask, "Have I done enough?" You ask, "What does the app say?"*

It would be naive, however, to dismiss gamification outright. When wisely applied, it can catalyse breakthroughs. Habitica, a to-do list crossed with a role-playing game, has helped users with ADHD stay organised. Zombies, Run! turns jogging into narrative immersion. These applications are not cynical—they are structured around user empowerment. The distinction lies in *intent and transparency*. Are the game elements designed to support human goals, or to sustain platform engagement? Do they disappear once no longer needed, or do they cling like scaffolding long after the structure is built?

Gamification thrives on abstraction. Complex activities—reading, learning, exercising—are reduced to discrete units that can be rewarded. But life does not always yield to abstraction. The most meaningful actions are often the least measurable: comforting a friend, changing one's mind, resisting a harmful habit. These are not badge-worthy, but they are the building blocks of character. *When everyday life is gamified, it becomes optimised for metrics, not morality; for output, not understanding.*

A more nuanced danger emerges when gamification intersects with social identity. Apps and platforms often display achievements publicly, transforming personal progress into social capital. The subtle message is that *you are what you can show*. This nudges behaviour from genuine to performative. You don't meditate to centre yourself—you do it to earn a badge or post a screenshot. You don't run to feel strong—you run to update your followers. The act is secondary to the artifact. *The reward becomes the ritual.*

Performance, when externalised, changes the performer. A phenomenon called "overjustification" shows that adding extrinsic rewards to an intrinsically motivated activity can reduce internal motivation over time. The joy of the activity is displaced by the pressure of the metric. Once the reward is removed, the behaviour may vanish. This is a particularly high cost in areas like education, fitness, or mental health—domains where sustainable habits matter more than momentary compliance.

The broader social implications are not trivial. A generation raised on gamified systems may come to expect reward for every action. This cultivates a fragile relationship with effort—one that demands immediate feedback, visible progress, and external validation. It undermines the development of *resilience,* which often depends on the ability to persist through invisible, unrewarded labour. It weakens the *moral imagination,* which depends on doing the right thing even when no one is watching.

We must ask: *What kind of people do these systems shape us into?* Not just in how we behave, but in how we think about action, meaning, and selfhood. A gamified life may be more productive, but is it more reflective? Is it more free? Or does it merely make us more legible to systems that reward conformity and performance?

This is not a call for Luddism. It is a call for design ethics. Gamification is not inherently manipulative, but it is never neutral. Designers make choices: what to reward, what to ignore, how to structure feedback, how to shape attention. These choices have cognitive, emotional, and even moral consequences. *They do not just influence what we do—they influence who we become.*

A more mature design philosophy would use gamification sparingly, provisionally, and with respect for user agency. It would foreground *reflection over reaction, depth over dopamine, process over product.* It would allow for failure, for ambiguity, for non-compliance. It would recognise that *not everything worth doing needs to be incentivised.* Some things matter because they matter. Not because they complete a ring, fill a bar, or light up a screen.

The challenge for the future is to reclaim motivation—not from technology, but from the habits it has formed in us. To act not because it will be rewarded, but because it aligns with what we value. To read without tracking, to run without logging, to learn without gamifying. *To remember that life, at its best, is not a game—but a practice.* One that deepens, not when points are scored, but when meaning is made.

Attention as Validation

One of the most consequential shifts in the architecture of self-worth over the past two decades has occurred so subtly that many scarcely noticed. Not through war or legislation, but through interface design and platform metrics, we have entered a psychological economy in which attention serves not merely as currency but as confirmation of existence. *You are what is seen, liked, commented on, and followed.* The affirmation of self, once the product of inner reflection or community feedback, is increasingly filtered through the countable, visible, and shareable. The machinery of digital platforms has not just captured attention—it has begun to define it.

Social media platforms were never neutral stages for human connection. From their inception, they were engineered around a core behavioural truth: *what gets measured, gets managed.* And what gets attention, gets replicated. The early shift from chronological timelines to algorithmic curation formalised this logic. Posts were ranked not by time but by engagement—likes, shares, dwell time, comments—establishing an invisible scoring system that quietly began to teach users what the platforms valued. These metrics became feedback loops. They shaped what we posted, how often we posted, and eventually, who we became in those digital spaces.

What emerged was a form of ambient behavioural training—subtle, persistent, and largely unacknowledged. Each notification, each red badge, each "like" acted as a dopamine trigger, reinforcing not only the action but the identity behind it. Neuroscientific studies confirm that these moments light up reward centres in the brain, particularly in adolescents and young adults. But unlike traditional rewards, which often come after sustained effort, digital feedback is often immediate and unpredictable—mirroring the neurological effect of gambling. The design is deliberate. Variable rewards are among the most addictive forms of reinforcement. *It is not the attention itself that changes us—it is the anticipation of it.*

Yet this shift is not simply about biology. It's about the slow recalibration of value. Historically, self-worth was grounded in personal development, social contribution, or enduring relationships. It was hard-won and often intangible. Today, these internal and interpersonal metrics are being displaced by the surface logic of platforms: visible engagement equals personal worth. An artwork that garners 10,000 likes is perceived as more meaningful than one that attracts 10—even if the latter represents years of effort and originality. A person with 50,000 followers is assumed to hold more cultural capital than one with 500, regardless of substance. *Attention becomes a proxy for merit—but a dangerously unreliable one.*

The consequences are not just individual but societal. When self-worth is externalised, identity becomes performative. The self is edited for visibility. People begin to post not what reflects who they are, but what performs well—what flatters the algorithm, what aligns with current sentiment, what avoids friction. This cultivates a culture of safety masquerading as authenticity. Ironically, the more one performs the "real" self, the less real it becomes. It is a carefully constructed persona built to optimise attention. *And when your value is determined by response, you begin to fear being ignored more than being misunderstood.*

This creates a precarious feedback loop. As validation is tethered to visibility, absence becomes erasure. You are not simply offline—you are irrelevant. The fear of missing out (FOMO) is no longer about experiences missed but about *being missed*. The fear is ontological. To be invisible is to be unimportant. This explains the compulsion to share continually, even when there's little to say. Not posting becomes a statement—sometimes interpreted as failure, decline, or withdrawal. In this climate, *silence is not golden; it is suspect.*

This feedback system also warps our understanding of time. Social media thrives on immediacy. A tweet that does not gain traction within the first hour is considered a dud. A post's lifespan is measured in minutes. This creates pressure to be constantly present, constantly producing, constantly responsive. Thoughtfulness, slowness, and ambiguity—traits essential to mature discourse—are penalised. In their place rise the quick take, the trending soundbite, the filtered image. *The rhythm of the self accelerates to match the tempo of the platform.*

There is also a class dynamic embedded in this system. The ability to generate engagement is not equally distributed. It favours those with photogenic lives, digital fluency, or platform privilege. This creates what philosopher Byung-Chul Han might describe as a "society of exhibition," where only certain types of selves are deemed worthy of attention. The metrics act not just as validation, but as gatekeepers. *What is visible becomes desirable; what is desirable becomes normative; what is normative becomes invisible to critique.*

What's lost in this attention calculus is the private self—the self that exists without applause, without documentation, without justification. This self is essential for resilience, creativity, and ethical development. It is where conviction forms, where ideas are tested, where failures are integrated. But in a landscape where everything is a potential post, even solitude becomes performable. "Taking a break" is itself announced. Even the retreat is narrated. *The audience is never fully dismissed.*

To understand the psychological toll of this, one must consider the distinction between *recognition* and *validation*. Recognition is mutual—it arises from being seen in one's complexity, by people who matter. Validation, in the digital sense, is transactional. It is a tap, a count, a signal that something about you aligns with expectations. But validation without recognition is empty. It affirms presence without understanding. *It feeds the ego but bypasses the self.*

Some have argued that this shift simply reflects a new form of sociality. That younger generations, raised on likes and stories, are developing novel ways of expressing and connecting. There is truth here. Not all attention-seeking is shallow; not all digital performance is inauthentic. But even this optimistic view must reckon with the costs. When the architecture of communication is built around visibility and speed, it rewards certain traits—extroversion, reactivity, conformity—and marginalises others. *Not everyone can thrive in the marketplace of attention.*

The structural pressures are not easily resisted. Many careers now depend on maintaining an online presence. Artists, academics, entrepreneurs, even therapists and scientists are advised to "build a brand." Visibility is not just validation—it is survival. This leads to a professionalisation of the self, where personal moments are curated for strategic gain. The result is exhaustion. The boundary between person and persona erodes. You're always "on," always optimising, always watching yourself being watched. *And when you are your own brand, rest feels like neglect.*

There is no simple antidote to this condition. Digital platforms are unlikely to abandon engagement metrics. They are too profitable, too embedded. But individuals and institutions can cultivate counterweights. We can resist the conflation of attention with value. We can build spaces—online or off—that reward depth over display, slowness over speed, substance over spectacle. *We can remember that being seen is not the same as being known.*

Ultimately, the question is existential. What is a self, if it is built on the reactions of strangers? What kind of society emerges when self-worth is measured in notifications? And what becomes of those who fail to perform—who are invisible, ambivalent, or simply tired? These are not abstract concerns. They shape the mental health of millions, the cohesion of communities, and the very texture of contemporary life. *If attention is the new validation, then we must ask: validated for what? And by whom?*

Reclaiming agency in this environment requires more than digital hygiene. It requires philosophical clarity. We must restore the distinction between performance and presence, between engagement and understanding, between affirmation and worth. Not to abandon technology, but to use it without being used by it. To be present in a world that monetises presence, and to remain whole in a system that rewards fragments. *To find value not in being seen, but in being real.*

Optics vs. Substance

A peculiar irony defines the digital age: while we now have unprecedented tools for self-expression, our sense of self is increasingly curated for others. The distinction between who we are and how we appear is no longer philosophical but operational. Platforms have made the visible self—the one that can be photographed, captioned, liked, and shared—not merely an extension of identity but often its primary performance. *Visibility becomes validation, and optics risk replacing substance as the defining currency of modern identity.*

This shift is not a superficial quirk of social media but a structural feature of the environments we inhabit. As sociologist Erving Goffman noted long before the internet, we are always managing impressions, adjusting behaviour depending on context. But digital platforms have industrialised this dynamic. They have made it measurable, persistent, and globally scalable. The stage is no longer the dinner party or the office—it is an endless feed, available 24/7 to any observer, real or algorithmic. *Performance is no longer temporary; it is archived.*

The implications are profound. When experiences are filtered through the lens of potential display, their intrinsic value is altered. A hike becomes a photo opportunity. A meal becomes content. A moment of stillness becomes a missed chance for a story. This is not merely a cultural annoyance—it is a cognitive shift. The question "What do I want to do?" is increasingly replaced by "What would this look like online?" In mediated spaces, *the logic of optics begins to precede the logic of authenticity.*

Nowhere is this more apparent than in the architecture of social media platforms themselves. Instagram, TikTok, and LinkedIn—despite wildly different tones—are united by a visual grammar that rewards polished presentation and penalises ambiguity. These platforms do not merely allow users to share; they shape *what* is shareable, by privileging that which is concise, attractive, and emotionally legible. The result is a self increasingly edited for consistency, clarity, and marketability. *Substance, which is often messy, complex, or slow, struggles to compete in such spaces.*

This tension is particularly acute in professional domains. The rise of the personal brand has collapsed traditional boundaries between private and public, between competence and charisma. A researcher is no longer judged solely by the rigour of their work, but by the clarity of their Twitter threads. An entrepreneur is not simply building a business but also cultivating an aesthetic. This trend is not inherently negative—clear communication and reach have value—but it risks creating a meritocracy of appearance, where *those who perform best often obscure those who do the best work.*

Even in activism and social causes, where sincerity and urgency are assumed, optics often dominate. A movement's traction can hinge less on organisational strength or policy acumen than on its hashtag visibility and aesthetic cohesion. Participation is increasingly performative—signalling alignment rather than enacting change. The concept of "virtue signalling," though often used dismissively, captures a real dynamic: *it is now easier to display values than to live them.*

This creates a double bind for individuals who are sincere. On the one hand, to be seen as credible or current, one must engage the optics of digital platforms. On the other, over-engagement risks reducing one's message—or self—to branding. Many users report a sense of split identity: the offline self, which feels nuanced and evolving, and the online self, which feels fixed and strategic. This psychological friction is subtle but draining. *The effort to appear authentic often erodes the very authenticity it seeks to project.*

It is tempting to dismiss these concerns as generational or aesthetic. But they speak to a deeper philosophical tension between being and seeming. The classical philosophers, from Plato to Kierkegaard, warned of the dangers of inauthentic living—of allowing external validation to define internal worth. What digital platforms have done is scale and monetise this vulnerability. They have turned *seeming* into a survival strategy, especially for those navigating competitive, hyper-visible environments.

Yet the tension between optics and substance is not binary. It is better understood as a spectrum of trade-offs. Visibility can amplify substance, but it can also dilute it. Consider the phenomenon of "Instagram poets" or "TikTok philosophers"—creators who gain rapid fame through digestible ideas. Some use this reach to introduce wider audiences to depth. Others flatten complexity to maintain relevance. The medium incentivises the latter. *Substance that cannot be packaged risks invisibility.*

This raises a critical question for institutions as well as individuals: how do we preserve depth in an attention economy optimised for surfaces? Universities, newsrooms, and cultural bodies increasingly feel the pressure to optimise their messaging for digital platforms. A well-researched report may generate less impact than a viral infographic. A nuanced documentary may lose ground to a 90-second reel. These are not just matters of marketing—they shape the very contours of what knowledge is produced and valued.

Even in intimate relationships, the divide between optics and substance is showing cracks. Couples stage moments of affection not for each other, but for followers. Families curate holiday albums with hashtags. Friendship becomes a performance of presence—measured in tags and comments, rather than calls and care. None of this is inherently false. But it points to a profound confusion of priorities. *When display becomes the metric of connection, connection itself is redefined.*

To navigate this terrain with integrity requires vigilance. It demands that we develop a personal and cultural literacy around the costs of display. This does not mean abandoning digital platforms, but interrogating their logic. It means asking not only what we are showing, but *why*. Is the post an expression or a performance? Is the message for others or a mask for ourselves? These questions, posed regularly, are acts of resistance.

There are, fortunately, emerging practices and subcultures that prioritise substance over optics. Long-form newsletters, closed communities, slow social platforms, and audio-first spaces such as podcasts all point to a hunger for depth. These spaces often sacrifice virality for connection, reach for richness. They are less about metrics and more about meaning. *They remind us that while optics dominate the mainstream, substance has not disappeared—it has simply migrated.*

Ultimately, the tension between living for self and living for display is not new—but its scale, speed, and psychological saturation are. We are all, to some degree, caught in the machinery of visibility. But there is still room for agency. Not in grand acts of withdrawal, but in small choices: resisting the urge to document everything, valuing what goes unseen, making peace with ambiguity, prioritising process over performance. *Because some of the most vital aspects of life—care, thought, growth—are hard to capture, and harder still to go viral.*

The question is not whether we will use digital platforms, but how we will live with them. Will we curate a life that looks good, or live one that feels good? Will we continue to measure worth by reach, or reclaim the quiet dignity of depth? These are not merely philosophical musings—they are design decisions, cultural decisions, ethical decisions. *In a world saturated with optics, choosing substance is not a retreat. It is a form of courage.*

Chapter 8
The Subtle Loss of Competence

It is entirely possible to navigate a day—or even a lifetime—without understanding how anything truly works. Today's individual can cross continents without consulting a map, dine lavishly without mastering a stove, communicate without spelling, calculate without arithmetic, and schedule without ever glancing at a clock. This is no speculative fiction; it is the lived experience of a world smoothed by technology, where friction is removed and tools anticipate our needs. Yet beneath this veneer of ease lies a subtle erosion. Convenience conceals decay; automation masks the quiet hollowing of human skill.

Competence has always meant more than mere utility. The ability to kindle a fire, repair clothing, bake bread, or draft a persuasive letter was never only functional—it was intimate knowledge, connecting people to the material world and rooting them in agency. As these tasks are gradually handed over to machines and interfaces, we do not simply outsource labour; we excise experiences that once formed the backbone of identity and self-reliance.

Consider mental arithmetic. For centuries, basic numeracy was essential, underpinning trade, budgeting, navigation, and negotiation. Today, calculators are not just tools but defaults, integrated into devices we carry constantly. Few question their utility. Yet when a person cannot roughly estimate a grocery bill or discern whether a discount is fair, something shifts. The decline of skill becomes a decline in intuitive judgment. Tools do not just replace effort; they reshape thought itself.

Memory, too, has been reconfigured. Remembering was once survival: addresses, phone numbers, directions, birthdays, historical facts, poetry—all committed to the mind out of necessity rather than nostalgia. Outsourcing memory to calendars, contacts, GPS, and search engines has diminished the perceived value of retention. But a remembered fact differs from one merely retrieved. Memory is contextual, reinforcing connections, priming associations, and deepening comprehension. To know something by heart is to carry it within oneself—not simply summon it on demand.

Navigation provides perhaps the clearest metaphor. Digital maps have revolutionised movement, yet dependence on GPS often undermines spatial awareness. Heavy users frequently exhibit weaker mental maps, arriving at destinations with little sense of geography. What is lost is not merely wayfinding but the felt relationship to space. The world becomes something traversed rather than inhabited.

These examples might seem trivial—does it matter if a child never learns cursive, or if a commuter cannot name the side streets of their own city? Yet competence is cumulative. The erosion of small skills creates larger vulnerabilities. When an ATM fails, an app crashes, or a system collapses, a deskilled individual is not merely inconvenienced—they are incapacitated. And the emotional toll exceeds frustration: it is helplessness. Dependence, when exposed, is disempowering.

This is not an argument against technology. Tools have always extended human capacity. The distinction lies between enhancement and replacement. A well-designed tool encourages mastery; it challenges and grows with its user. A convenience tool, by contrast, minimises involvement, delivering outcomes without comprehension. Gradually, the human role shifts from agent to recipient. The loss is not merely of skill but of confidence.

Photography illustrates this clearly. The leap from film to smartphone has made image-making ubiquitous. Yet craft has narrowed. Autofocus, auto-exposure, preset filters, facial recognition—all reduce the photographer to pointing and tapping. The images may be crisp, but the user may no longer grasp light, depth, or framing. The camera is clever; the user becomes passive. Skill becomes selection rather than creation.

Cooking offers a parallel. Recipe apps, meal kits, and kitchen gadgets simplify preparation. The gains are tangible—less time, less waste, greater consistency. Yet when techniques go unlearned—judging heat, seasoning intuitively, improvising with available ingredients—dependency grows. Following instructions replaces understanding. Real cooking is responsive: to ingredients, taste, memory. Without that responsiveness, a meal nourishes the body but not the self.

Even the banal act of scheduling reveals the divide. Calendars now sync automatically: meetings are set, reminders optimised, conflicts flagged. In this hyper-efficiency, users no longer cultivate temporal intuition. They are told where to be and when. The day is served rather than shaped.

Such shifts raise a fundamental question: what role does difficulty play in human development? In automating challenge, are we anaesthetising growth? Historically, acquiring skill was never merely functional; it was formative. Difficulty taught patience, effort, failure, and correction. These experiences, often frustrating, conferred pride. Mastery, hard-won, derived meaning from its challenge. When tasks are frictionless, that meaning often evaporates.

Moreover, skill confers authority. Knowledge enables judgment, intervention, and adaptation. Competence underpins autonomy; it anchors decision-making. A deskilled person may function, yet within constraints imposed by designers, algorithms, or vendors. Their life becomes navigable but not steerable.

This matters acutely in crisis. When systems fail—through disaster, disruption, or upheaval—competence is survival, not luxury. Even outside crisis, it sustains dignity. A child tying their shoes, a worker repairing tools, a retiree tending a garden—all express independence, however modest. They assert identity through capability rather than consumption.

This is not nostalgia, nor a call to reject modern tools. Rather, it is a plea for recalibration. Where does automation serve, and where does it diminish? Which skills merit preservation—not for necessity alone, but for their role in shaping character? Can systems be designed to invite participation rather than merely deliver outcomes?

The argument is not against progress, but against amnesia. When we no longer need to do something, we risk forgetting why it mattered. Ease may masquerade as excellence; reliance, as advancement. But the quiet truth remains: we value what we can do ourselves. In knowing, making, mastering, we locate ourselves in the world. Surrender that knowledge entirely, and the loss is personal. It is the erosion of presence, of confidence, of identity.

As tools continue to accelerate and abstract our lives, the questions must remain: what do they save us from—and what do they quietly take away along the way?

What We No Longer Need to Know

When tools advance far enough, they begin to delete not only difficulty but the very memory of difficulty. The astonishing efficiency of modern systems—digital maps that guide every turn, predictive text that completes our thoughts, calculators that answer before we've begun to solve—has not merely made certain skills optional. It has rendered them invisible. We live amid an unprecedented shift in human cognition: a *redefinition of what counts as worth knowing*. Not by decree, but by slow omission. And what fades is not trivial. It includes the foundational skills that once shaped how we thought, decided, and related to the world.

Mental arithmetic is among the clearest examples. There was a time not long ago when estimating a tip, calculating a discount, or even balancing a cheque book required cognitive effort. Not advanced mathematics—just mental fluency with numbers. Today, this baseline skill is rarely exercised, not due to laziness, but because there is no pressing need. Digital devices perform these functions instantly and without friction. The result is that we often forget how to do what we once considered elementary. But what we lose is not just calculation—it is a kind of mental nimbleness. *Mental arithmetic sharpens estimation, reinforces number sense, and supports logical reasoning*. Its decline is not neutral. It narrows cognitive elasticity.

Navigation follows a similar trajectory. GPS-based systems have revolutionised mobility, reducing the cognitive burden of wayfinding to almost zero. You can land in a foreign city, enter a destination, and follow instructions with no understanding of orientation, scale, or spatial relationships. You will likely reach your target. But you will not know how you got there. Nor will you be able to reconstruct the route without the device. Over time, this shifts navigation from *a mental model of the environment* to *a procedural task of obedience*. What fades is not only the map in the mind, but also a more general *sense of directional agency*—the confidence of knowing where one stands and how to get elsewhere unaided.

The decline of handwriting is less discussed but similarly revealing. Typing, voice-to-text, and touchscreen input dominate. Yet handwriting is not merely an older modality—it is a distinct cognitive process. Neuroscience has consistently shown that forming letters by hand activates memory, motor control, and conceptual encoding in ways that typing does not. This is particularly true in children, where handwriting supports deeper learning and idea formation. But even for adults, writing longhand slows thought to a more reflective pace. It creates a physical imprint of thinking. When handwriting disappears, *so does a form of embodied cognition.* Communication may become faster, but thought becomes thinner.

Face-to-face negotiation, too, is quietly eroding. In a world of text-based customer service, email threads, and algorithmically priced platforms, the space for human persuasion shrinks. Once, negotiating a price, resolving a complaint, or advocating for oneself required reading expressions, adjusting tone, and deploying rhetoric. It required emotional calibration and improvisation. Now, much of this terrain is pre-empted by fixed pricing, chatbots, or silent rejection. The effect is dual: people lose the opportunity to practice persuasive communication, and systems become resistant to it. As the need for negotiation wanes, so too does *our comfort with interpersonal uncertainty*. We become fluent in transactions, but not in negotiation—precisely the skill that builds both empathy and assertiveness.

What unites these shifts is not technological change itself, but *the narrowing of cognitive participation*. We are no longer expected to do things that were once foundational to competence. More subtly, we are not expected to remember how to do them. This is not a lament for a bygone era. It is a reflection on *what knowledge for its own sake once conferred.* The skill of doing something oneself, even when a faster option exists, shapes one's sense of agency. It grants independence, cultivates judgment, and builds trust in one's own mind.

Consider the act of remembering. To retain a phone number, a schedule, or a friend's address is now viewed as inefficient, even quaint. Why bother when everything is stored for you? Yet *remembering is not redundant.* It strengthens neural connections. It builds associative networks. A remembered fact is more readily applied, more deeply felt, and more likely to be integrated into broader understanding. Forgetting how to remember is not simply a logistical risk—it is a cognitive impoverishment. We come to *know less not only about the world but about how we know.*

There is also a psychological dimension to this erosion. As tasks are increasingly performed for us, our internal narrative shifts from "I can do this" to "I hope this works." The locus of control moves outward. A misbehaving GPS is blamed for tardiness. A calendar glitch justifies a missed meeting. An autocorrect error explains a miscommunication. These are small deflections, but cumulatively they point to a mindset of *externalised responsibility*. Over time, this corrodes confidence. If one cannot reliably perform without tools, one begins to distrust one's own capabilities—even when the task is simple.

This erosion is particularly perilous for younger generations. When tools are introduced before mastery, skill acquisition is never fully achieved. A child who learns to spell with autocorrect, navigate with GPS, and socialise through messaging may never develop the internal scaffolding those tools replaced. And without that scaffolding, there is no fallback. The tool fails; the user is stranded. This is not speculation—it is visible in the classroom, the workplace, and beyond. Increasingly, people are *technologically fluent but cognitively brittle*. They can operate systems but cannot improvise without them.

To understand the deeper cost of what we no longer need to know, we must examine the role of redundancy in learning. Historically, skills were acquired not solely for their daily utility, but as part of a repertoire of preparedness. One might not need to do long division every day, but knowing how grounded one's mathematical literacy. Similarly, one might not need to negotiate regularly, but having done so instilled a kind of *social muscle*. These redundancies acted as buffers—absorbing shocks, providing options, allowing adaptation. As redundancy is stripped away in the name of efficiency, so too is *resilience.*

Yet the issue is not binary. It is not a question of choosing between the manual and the digital. The real challenge is *how to preserve the virtues of competence in an environment that makes competence optional.* This is both a design problem and a cultural one. Can tools be structured to encourage participation rather than passivity? Can we value knowing how, even when we don't have to? Can educational systems teach not just how to use tools, but *how to think independently of them*?

There are promising countercurrents. The resurgence of interest in handwriting among students, the rise of "slow tech" movements, the popularity of mental fitness apps that challenge memory and logic—these suggest a latent recognition that something is slipping. But such efforts remain marginal. The dominant design of our digital world rewards ease over understanding. And in that trade, it is often hard to see what is vanishing—because what disappears is not loud. It is quiet, cumulative, and *undetectable until tested.*

The question, then, is not whether technology makes life better. It clearly does. The question is: *What are we becoming unable to do without it?* And do we notice, care, or prepare for that gap? When we no longer need to know certain things, we may forget how knowing once shaped us. And in that forgetting, we risk not just losing skills, but misplacing parts of ourselves.

Knowledge, after all, is not only power. It is presence. It is the subtle self-assurance that comes from having more than one way to approach a problem. More than one route through a city. More than one voice in a conversation. And the capacity to choose—not merely to follow. That is what fades when we stop needing to know. Not just the facts, but the *freedom they once enabled.*

Deskilling and Dependence

It is a peculiar feature of progress that as the tools around us become more capable, we, their users, often become less so. The original promise of technology—amplifying human ability—has quietly shifted from enhancement to replacement. As tasks are outsourced to apps, platforms, and systems, the skills those tasks once required begin to wither. This is not a hypothetical worry or nostalgic lament; it is a measurable, structural phenomenon. *Deskilling is not a side effect—it is a design outcome.* And the longer it continues unnoticed, the more it shapes what people can do, what they are willing to try, and who they believe themselves to be.

The fundamental issue is not that people have fewer skills than their ancestors. Every era sheds certain practices. The problem is *the mechanism by which skills are lost today*. In the past, skills decayed because they were no longer relevant. Candle-making declined with the rise of electric light. Horse-riding waned when cars became common. But in the digital age, skills are not phased out because their use disappears. They decline *while still being contextually valuable*. People can still benefit from reading a map, calculating a percentage, remembering a fact, or holding a difficult conversation. But when a system does it for them, they do it less. Then they stop doing it altogether. Eventually, they no longer *can*.

Navigation offers a vivid case. GPS applications are among the most widely used digital tools, offering turn-by-turn directions that relieve users of the need to understand geography. In 2013, researchers from McGill University published findings that frequent GPS use was associated with reduced activity in the hippocampus—a brain region essential for spatial memory and orientation. Participants who navigated manually showed greater engagement in route learning, mental mapping, and memory recall. Those who followed GPS instructions, by contrast, engaged in *passive movement*. The cognitive load was lower, but so too was the mental imprint. Navigation became a task of obedience, not understanding.

This form of cognitive displacement—wherein a tool performs a function, and the brain defers to it—is now widespread. Spellcheck corrects our writing before we've registered the mistake. Predictive text completes our sentences before we've fully thought them. Smart fridges remind us to buy milk. These tools remove friction, but they also *remove memory cues, attentional practice, and problem-solving exercises.* The result is not simply convenience—it is a rewiring of how effort is distributed. And where there is no effort, there is no learning. *Competence decays fastest when it feels least needed.*

The insidious nature of deskilling lies in its gradualness. Unlike a traumatic loss of ability, such as forgetting how to drive, deskilling is imperceptible until it is tested. A person reliant on voice-to-text input may not realise they can no longer spell common words. Someone who always checks restaurant reviews may forget how to trust their own judgment. These examples are not dramatic, but they are *cumulative*. And over time, they compromise a person's ability to function independently.

The shift from enhancement to dependence is also tied to how tools are designed. Most consumer technologies today are not passive instruments; they are *active systems*, optimised for outcomes, not understanding. Take the example of modern photography. A smartphone camera, with AI-powered focus, lighting adjustment, and facial recognition, produces stunning images. But the user learns little about exposure, composition, or shutter speed. The machine handles those variables silently, invisibly. Over time, photography shifts from *a skill to a button*. The user becomes a curator, not a creator. They rely on algorithms to judge quality, not their own eye.

This dynamic is mirrored in cooking. Meal kits with pre-measured ingredients and step-by-step instructions simplify the process, but they also constrain experimentation. A person following the app is unlikely to learn how to adjust seasoning, salvage a dish, or innovate based on what's in the fridge. They become *good at following*, not good at cooking. And if the system breaks down—if the app crashes, or the instructions are wrong—they are stranded.

Even calendar management, a seemingly innocuous domain, illustrates the same pattern. Scheduling tools can auto-suggest meeting times, account for time zones, and integrate multiple calendars. But with heavy reliance comes *an erosion of temporal literacy*. People become less aware of how long tasks take, less skilled at estimating buffers, and more dependent on prompts. Scheduling becomes reactive. And with it, a deeper capacity—the ability to organise one's time meaningfully—atrophies.

This matters because skills are not just utilities; they are forms of cognition. When people cook, navigate, write, or remember, they engage neural pathways that affect reasoning, confidence, and creativity. To lose a skill is not just to outsource a function—it is to forgo a mode of thinking. *Tools change not only what we do, but how we think about doing*.

Crucially, the argument here is not technophobic. Tools can and should enhance human capacity. The printing press, the calculator, and the spreadsheet all extended what was possible. The question is whether today's tools *cultivate latent ability or bypass it*. Do they strengthen the user, or supplant them? Enhancement implies partnership. Dependence implies substitution.

Consider the concept of muscle memory. Athletes and musicians speak of practice embedding itself in the body, such that action becomes fluid, intuitive. Something similar applies to cognitive skills. Mental flexibility, strategic thinking, and decision-making all improve with repetition and effort. But if effort is consistently diverted—to devices, prompts, or pre-set options—then the brain *does not consolidate* those patterns. It becomes less sure of its own capacity. This is why deskilling is not just a performance issue; it is a *psychological one*. When people stop believing they can do things, they lose more than skill—they lose *agency*.

This has real-world implications. In professional contexts, over-reliance on automation can erode judgement. A financial analyst who accepts the algorithm's recommendation without interrogation may fail to notice an anomaly. A doctor who leans too heavily on diagnostic software may overlook context-specific factors. In aviation, over-trust in autopilot systems has been cited in several accidents where pilots were ill-equipped to resume manual control under duress. These are extreme cases, but they illustrate the same pattern: *when tools become dominant, the human role becomes secondary*. And when that happens, skills degrade silently, until they are needed—and absent.

There is also a deeper philosophical concern. Skills provide more than function; they provide *identity*. To be skilled is to know, to trust, to act. A culture that prizes frictionless interfaces and plug-and-play solutions risks hollowing out the very capacities that give individuals meaning. To be replaced, even subtly, is to be diminished. Not because the tool is evil, but because the skill—the self—was never allowed to develop alongside it.

The way forward is not to reject tools but to design with foresight. Systems can be created that *invite participation rather than automate exclusion*. Consider the re-emergence of mechanical watches as status symbols. Their appeal lies not in precision—quartz is more accurate—but in craftsmanship, complexity, and *the pleasure of manual engagement*. Likewise, educational tools that challenge users to solve before revealing answers encourage cognitive growth. Even GPS apps that show the map and ask for confirmation—rather than blind following—support spatial learning. These are small shifts, but they respect the user's mind.

Ultimately, the issue is not whether people need to perform every task manually. It is whether they retain *the capacity and confidence to do so*. Deskilling is not dangerous because it makes us slower or less efficient. It is dangerous because it detaches us from our own potential. And once detached, people become passive in their own lives—waiting for the prompt, the option, the update. That is not merely technological dependence. *It is a shrinking of the human role* in a world increasingly run by machines.

Reclaiming skill does not mean rejecting convenience. It means recognising that *not every shortcut is worth taking*. Some paths must be walked, not because they are efficient, but because they teach us how to walk. In the end, tools should elevate us, not replace us. And that elevation begins with a simple question: *What am I still capable of, unaided?* The more often we answer it honestly, the less likely we are to lose what matters.

Automation vs. Mastery

There is an unquestioned assumption embedded in much of our technological progress: if something can be automated, it should be. The pursuit of efficiency, once the hallmark of industrial logic, has infiltrated daily life, repackaging friction as failure and effort as inefficiency. Automation now touches nearly every sphere—from how we cook dinner, to how we plan meetings, to how we capture the world around us through a lens. And yet, *not all tasks are made better by being easier*. Some are made worse. Because what we save in labour, we may quietly lose in meaning.

The distinction between labour-saving and meaning-saving is neither semantic nor nostalgic. It marks the boundary between convenience that liberates, and convenience that hollows out. Not all human activity is valuable because it is efficient. Much of what we consider enriching—creative work, problem-solving, skill-building—*derives its meaning from the doing*, not just the outcome. A perfectly prepared meal is satisfying, but the act of preparing it—judging flavours, adjusting seasoning, coordinating timing—creates a form of engagement that automation cannot replicate. The same is true of photography and scheduling: mastery in these domains comes not from outcome alone, but from *understanding, effort, and nuance.*

Photography is among the most vivid illustrations of this tension. The modern smartphone, with its array of AI-powered features, has made it nearly impossible to take a bad photo. The camera detects faces, balances exposure, sharpens edges, and even recommends framing. A child can now produce images that, a decade ago, required a professional. Technologically, this is a triumph. But what it enables in output, it displaces in learning. The relationship between aperture and depth of field, the tactile awareness of shutter speed, the eye for light and composition—these no longer develop through practice, because they are no longer necessary for results.

Yet those skills are not arbitrary. They are *the very medium of photographic literacy*. A photographer who understands the mechanics of their tool is better able to shape their vision, improvise in imperfect conditions, and express intent. Mastery gives access to subtleties automation cannot read. A sunset filtered through haze, a portrait under mixed lighting, a deliberate motion blur—these are not defects to be corrected by software. They are choices. When the machine removes friction by default, it also removes the possibility of those choices. And what remains is not mastery, but compliance: point, shoot, and accept what the algorithm decides is best.

A parallel trend unfolds in the kitchen. Services like meal kits, smart ovens, and AI-recommended recipes reduce the complexity of cooking into highly guided steps. This is a gift for the time-poor or the culinary novice. But it often comes at the expense of *culinary judgement.* Cooking used to be an apprenticeship in intuition. One learned by smell, texture, sound—the subtle indicators that a dish was progressing well or veering off course. These signals demanded presence, awareness, adaptation. With automation, those feedback loops are replaced by instruction: heat to this temperature, stir for this time, stop when prompted.

What disappears in that transition is *improvisational confidence.* The ability to adapt a recipe to missing ingredients, to recover a sauce gone thin, to season a dish without measuring—is not a luxury. It is what separates someone who can *follow* from someone who can *create.* The automation of food preparation threatens not just a skill but a culture of agency: the idea that a person can look at a set of ingredients and build a meal from instinct. Cooking, like all crafts, is an interplay between structure and imagination. And when structure becomes rigid, imagination has nowhere to go.

Scheduling may seem like an unlikely domain for this conversation, but it, too, reveals how automation can displace understanding. Digital calendars now predict optimal meeting times, account for time zones, avoid conflicts, and suggest durations. These features remove significant cognitive load—but also weaken *temporal intuition.* A person accustomed to algorithmic scheduling may struggle to estimate task length, anticipate overrun, or evaluate how meetings affect their energy and focus. Time becomes a series of slots filled by software, rather than a rhythm shaped by discernment.

This is not a sentimental argument for manual scheduling. It is a reminder that *calendars are not just logistical tools—they are expressions of priorities.* Mastery over one's schedule implies the ability to think strategically about time: when to create, when to reflect, when to rest. It is a discipline that develops through active engagement with one's commitments. When that engagement is replaced by automation, the user is less a planner than a participant—responding to invitations, adjusting to prompts, but no longer setting the tempo. Over time, this breeds not efficiency, but *passivity*.

What ties these examples together is a conceptual pivot: *Automation saves labour. Mastery generates meaning.* And these two goals, while not always at odds, are often in tension. Tools designed to minimise friction can also minimise attention. Tasks that once required presence—reading cues, making decisions, learning through error—become interactions of compliance. The user follows the path of least resistance, because that is what the tool rewards. And with each iteration, the activity becomes less a craft and more a service. The joy of doing is replaced by the ease of having it done.

The consequences of this shift are cultural as much as personal. In a society that privileges results above all, mastery becomes undervalued. Why spend hours learning to bake when a machine can do it better? Why understand composition when filters can beautify any photo? Why learn to manage your calendar when AI can do it on your behalf? These are not unreasonable questions—but they are built on a narrow premise: *that the only value worth pursuing is output*. The deeper truth is that some things are worth doing *because of how they change us in the doing*.

There is also a psychological cost to over-automation. Mastery is not just about skill—it is about identity. People derive confidence, satisfaction, and purpose from knowing they are capable. When tools remove the need to try, they often remove the opportunity to grow. A person who never learns to cook feels helpless in a kitchen. A person who cannot explain how their schedule came together is less likely to question it. A person who depends entirely on automatic settings may begin to mistrust their own judgement. The tool was meant to assist. But *when it usurps*, it diminishes.

That said, the goal is not to reject automation outright. It is to ask better questions about where and how it is applied. Automation should support mastery, not replace it. A camera that helps a photographer explore new techniques. A recipe app that encourages improvisation. A scheduling tool that visualises time to improve planning. These are examples of *augmentative design*—technologies that strengthen the user's capabilities rather than displace them. They honour the principle that *some tasks are worth understanding even if they can be delegated.*

There is a deeper philosophical thread that undergirds all of this. Mastery is a form of human flourishing. It reflects the belief that people can, with time and effort, become skilled in the world. Automation, when poorly applied, short-circuits that journey. It promises immediate results, but those results are hollow if they require no investment, no practice, no growth. And this is where the distinction between labour-saving and meaning-saving becomes urgent. *A society obsessed with frictionlessness may find itself surrounded by tools—but devoid of skills.*

To reclaim the value of mastery is not to resist technology, but to re-centre human capability within it. It is to design for participation, not just consumption. To build tools that educate as they assist. And to remember that *the path to excellence is often the path of effort.* There is a reason why people still learn instruments, despite streaming music. Why they take photographs with film, despite megapixels. Why they knead dough by hand, despite breadmakers. These acts are not irrational—they are *expressions of care, curiosity, and the quiet dignity of knowing how.*

The real measure of progress is not how much work we can eliminate, but how much agency we can preserve. And that agency begins with understanding what we are doing, why it matters, and how we might do it better next time. Automation may be inevitable. But mastery is optional. And in that option lies a choice about what kind of lives we want to lead. Not just faster, easier, or more efficient—but richer, deeper, and more fully human.

Competence as Confidence

There is a quiet erosion taking place—not of intelligence, but of confidence. Not of access to information, but of trust in our own ability to act on it. In a world increasingly optimised for delegation, automation, and passive convenience, something vital is slipping beneath the surface: *the intrinsic security that comes from knowing how to do things yourself.* This is not merely a nostalgic lament for bygone skills. It is a deeper argument—that *competence is foundational to agency*, and that when it atrophies, so too does the architecture of personal dignity and autonomy.

Competence is not just the ability to complete a task. It is *the capacity to navigate uncertainty with grounded knowledge*. It is what allows someone to walk into a situation, assess it independently, and make decisions without constant deferral to external systems or experts. Whether it's assembling a piece of furniture without a step-by-step video, having a difficult conversation without a script, or troubleshooting a stalled car without panic, competence *anchors the self* in a way no app or shortcut can replicate. It is, at its core, a form of intellectual and emotional sovereignty.

The modern landscape, however, increasingly rewards the opposite. We are surrounded by tools that absorb not just effort, but also *understanding*. Navigation apps tell us where to go but not how to read the terrain. Grammar-checking software corrects our writing without teaching us why the rule matters. Voice assistants deliver answers, but rarely context. Over time, this repeated outsourcing of know-how breeds an internal passivity—*a learned helplessness cloaked in convenience*. The individual may remain high-functioning, even productive, but their confidence becomes brittle, reliant on the uninterrupted performance of systems they cannot explain or repair.

This phenomenon is most visible in moments of system failure. When the satnav disconnects, the power goes out, or the software crashes, the unprepared user is thrust into a kind of cognitive vertigo. What once would have been a minor inconvenience now feels existential. There is an eerie vulnerability in not knowing how to proceed without technological scaffolding. *True confidence, by contrast, comes from resilience*—the calm assurance that even when tools fail, skills remain.

To understand why competence fosters confidence, it helps to recognise the way skill development shapes identity. When we learn how to do something—particularly something complex or nuanced—we do not merely add a utility to our mental toolbox. We *reshape how we see ourselves*. A person who learns how to fix a leaky tap no longer sees plumbing as foreign territory. A student who masters statistical analysis no longer sees data as abstract noise. Each skill acquired becomes a lens through which the world appears less opaque and more navigable. Competence *shrinks fear and expands possibility*.

The opposite is also true. A life over-indexed on delegation creates a distorted relationship with one's own abilities. This is not a matter of laziness or lack of intelligence. Often, it is an unintended consequence of affluence or abundance—why learn to change a tyre when roadside assistance is minutes away? Why study tax law when an app can file your return in three clicks? The problem is not in the tools themselves, but in the unconscious shift in mindset they encourage: *from capability to dependency*. The more we automate without understanding, the more the world begins to feel like a black box—useful, but unreadable. And when we feel unable to read the world, we become more anxious, more deferential, and less willing to act without permission or instruction.

Consider how this manifests in professional environments. In workplaces where employees are trained only to follow protocols, rather than understand the underlying systems, you find a fragile form of efficiency. People can perform well when things go as expected. But when uncertainty arises, or rules clash, or judgement is required, *confidence collapses*. The competent worker, by contrast, is not merely someone who can complete tasks; they are someone who understands enough to improvise, adapt, and question. Competence breeds not just confidence, but *discernment*—the ability to know when to push back, when to redesign, when to escalate, and when to solve the problem themselves.

This principle also carries deep psychological implications. Numerous studies in behavioural science suggest that *self-efficacy*—the belief in one's own competence—is one of the strongest predictors of resilience, motivation, and mental wellbeing. People who believe they can influence outcomes are more likely to persist in the face of obstacles, take initiative, and recover from setbacks. By contrast, individuals who doubt their competence tend to experience higher stress, decision paralysis, and burnout. In this light, competence is not merely a practical skillset; it is *the emotional infrastructure of agency*.

Education offers a compelling lens through which to view the slow erosion of competence. As digital aids proliferate, students often learn in environments where struggle is pathologised and immediate results are prioritised. But struggle is the crucible in which competence is forged. A student who wrestles with a problem, explores multiple solutions, and finally arrives at understanding experiences a transformation that no answer key can replicate. That moment of self-earned clarity becomes *a private source of strength*, one that accumulates over time. The classroom, then, is not just a place to acquire facts—it is where young people begin to *build the internal scaffolding of capability*.

The decline of competence has cultural dimensions as well. In societies where status is defined by consumption rather than creation, by output rather than understanding, *doing it yourself becomes a marker of frugality rather than skill*. The builder, the craftsperson, the mechanic—once admired for their autonomy—are often overlooked in favour of the manager, the influencer, the strategist. Yet in times of crisis or disruption, it is precisely these foundational competencies that prove most valuable. During the early months of the COVID-19 pandemic, for instance, people rediscovered the value of knowing how to cook, grow food, sew masks, and manage their own time. *Crisis exposes dependency; competence buffers it.*

One of the more subtle benefits of competence is that it reduces the need for constant validation. A person who knows they can do something well does not require applause for doing it. This contrasts sharply with the performative culture that emerges when competence is lacking—where effort must be documented, shared, and liked in order to feel real. The more confident a person is in their own abilities, the less they need external affirmation to reinforce their worth. This is not a call to stoicism, but a reminder that *quiet mastery often outlasts loud display*.

There is also a democratic dimension to competence. A population that knows how things work—how to cook food, repair homes, manage finances, navigate bureaucracies—is harder to manipulate. *Competence decentralises power.* It creates citizens who can think critically, act independently, and participate in decisions that affect them. By contrast, a public that is perpetually dependent on institutions or experts for every function of life becomes pliable. The erosion of competence, then, is not just a personal loss—it is *a civic vulnerability*.

What, then, does it mean to design for competence in a world increasingly geared toward convenience? It does not mean rejecting technology or fetishising manual labour. It means *building tools and systems that teach as they assist*. It means creating educational environments that reward process as much as result. It means encouraging workplaces that develop skill, not just compliance. And it means fostering a culture that respects the person who knows how to do things—not just the one who knows how to talk about them.

Ultimately, competence is a quiet form of power. It is the difference between waiting and acting, between hoping and doing. It may not show up in resumes or social media profiles, but it shows up when it matters: when something breaks, when the plan changes, when no one else knows what to do. To be competent is to know, deeply and calmly, that you have what it takes—not just to function, but to respond. That confidence is not loud, but it is unmistakable. It is not about being the best, but about *knowing enough to begin*. And in a world full of noise, distraction, and dependency, that may be the most valuable skill of all.

Chapter 9
Designing for Drift

Most people do not wake up intending to spend hours scrolling through feeds, chasing streaks, or tapping "next episode." And yet, somehow, that is exactly what happens. This is not merely a byproduct of convenience or ubiquity. Digital tools are deliberately crafted to capture attention, subtly nudge behaviour, and reshape intentions without overt force. We speak of "using" technology as though mastery rests with the user—but increasingly, it is the user who obeys the system. Not through coercion, but through gradual, almost imperceptible drift: small behavioural shifts accumulated over time, orchestrated beneath conscious awareness.

At the heart of this drift lies a principle of asymmetrical intention. Users arrive with their own goals—connection, learning, entertainment, productivity. Platforms, however, operate on an entirely different metric: retention, monetisation, and the extraction of behavioural data. This misalignment is not trivial. It produces a quiet tension between perception and reality. When Netflix autoplay nudges the next episode, or Instagram refreshes promising a dopamine hit, the interaction feels seamless, even delightful. Yet these conveniences are far from accidental; they are finely calibrated incentives, designed not to serve the user, but to optimise engagement metrics.

These incentives live not in the content itself but in the architecture of the interface. As Tristan Harris, former Google design ethicist, has emphasised, persuasive technology is not passive. Colours, timing, and micro-rewards—the red notification badge, the delay of a message, the psychology of a "like"—each carries a macro-intention. The result is not blunt coercion but structured seduction: an environment that subtly directs behaviour while preserving the illusion of autonomy.

Persuasion is not inherently problematic—communication always persuades. The challenge arises when design becomes invisible. We easily recognise manipulation from a salesperson, yet rarely from an interface. Infinite scroll, for example, is not an emergent feature of human behaviour; it was deliberately patented in 2006 by Aza Raskin as a method to sustain engagement. Its absence of friction was designed, not discovered, and quickly became the industry norm, reinforcing an operational ethos: maximise attention, regardless of cognitive cost.

Influence through design is not new. Behavioural economists from Richard Thaler to Daniel Kahneman have long studied "choice architecture," the way environments shape decisions. Digital environments, however, differ fundamentally: they are dynamic, adaptive, and algorithmically tuned. A supermarket may place sweets by the till; Facebook recalibrates that till for each user in real time, analysing past clicks, emotional tone, engagement frequency, and countless other signals. This is not static nudging—it is ongoing behavioural sculpting, executed by systems that often understand our preferences better than we do.

The consequences extend beyond mere distraction. Tools initially meant for expression become arenas for performance; platforms intended to inform become instruments of validation. Over time, users do not merely behave differently—they change. Subtle, persistent cues shape desires and priorities, aligning the logic of the self with the logic of the platform. Attention fragments, values shift, and what the system rewards becomes the compass by which we navigate.

Take "stories" on Snapchat or Instagram, for instance: ephemeral posts that vanish after 24 hours. They seem harmless, even liberating—post without permanence. Yet they cultivate habitual checking, fear of missing out, and compulsive maintenance of a digital persona. The incentive is unmistakable: remain visible or risk fading from awareness. This is social maintenance masquerading as interaction, structured to optimise user return rather than enrichment.

These mechanisms are often justified under the banner of "user experience." But whose experience truly matters? The answer lies in the business model: platforms monetising attention through advertising prioritise presence, clickability, and emotional priming over well-being. Nir Eyal's Hooked framework outlines the familiar loop: trigger, action, reward, investment. Habits form naturally, yet when these loops are deployed without reflection or accountability, they redefine user goals, often subtly.

Few users perceive this redefinition, because persuasive design rarely feels intrusive. The interface is infinite, the content flat, the user isolated. Beneath this surface hums a complex architecture indifferent to individuality—interested only in clicks. And in that reduction, aspects of the human experience are quietly compressed.

Design is never neutral. Every feature carries an implicit value system. A feed privileging recency over depth promotes ephemerality; one privileging controversy over nuance promotes outrage. These are not incidental effects—they reflect what the system values, and by extension, what it trains the user to value. The interface itself becomes ideology.

Not all persuasive technology is harmful. Behavioural insights can support health, learning, or habit formation. But ethical design demands transparency: users should know not just what the system does, but what it seeks to achieve. They must retain the power to override, resist, or opt out when necessary.

The pressing design challenge today is not additional features, but intentionality. How can systems help users align actions with their own values rather than bending values to fit platform incentives? How can interfaces reveal their logic instead of obscuring it? How can friction be introduced—not as obstruction, but as a pause for reflection?

Addressing these questions requires a new type of designer—one attentive not only to pixels but to people, not only to flows but to ethics, not only to engagement but to alignment. It demands a new type of user as well: one who interrogates the tool rather than unconsciously absorbing defaults. Designing for drift is the consequence of metric-driven creation absent moral scrutiny. Designing against drift demands clarity, care, and a commitment to preserving human agency within persuasive environments.

This chapter confronts a discomfiting reality: most digital platforms are engineered not to support intention, but to divert it. Blaming algorithms or lamenting addictive behaviour is insufficient. Understanding drift—the way it is designed, concealed, and internalised—is essential. Only by recognising how platforms shape not just action, but selfhood, can we aspire to design for integrity: for tools that remember they are instruments, and users who remember they remain free to choose.

Invisible Intentions

Most technology platforms are not in the business of giving users what they want. They are in the business of directing users toward behaviours that serve the platform's incentives—engagement, monetisation, data extraction, growth. Yet this divergence is rarely noticed because the mechanics that orchestrate it are embedded in design, not declared in text. Interfaces do not disclose their motives; they *suggest* them. They nudge, delay, highlight, and hide. And in doing so, they gradually reshape not only how users behave, but how they *decide what matters*. The real power of digital systems lies not in the tools they provide, but in the incentives they encode—what they reward, suppress, count, and make invisible.

Consider a commonplace action: opening a social media app. The user's intention may be to check on a friend, post a thought, or pass time while waiting in line. The platform's intention is different: to maximise time spent, increase ad exposure, and gather behavioural data. These intentions are not mutually exclusive, but they are asymmetrical. And over time, the platform's incentive begins to bend the user's intention. Scrolling becomes habitual. Likes become goals. Time becomes elastic. The user does not notice that their original purpose has drifted, because the interface is frictionless—smooth by design, cognitively invisible.

What makes this dynamic so insidious is that *the user believes they are in control*. The illusion of agency is preserved. You choose to scroll. You choose to click. But what you are shown, how it is ranked, how much friction exists to leave—all of that is preconfigured to align with platform goals. Tech critic and former Google employee James Williams captures this succinctly: "The liberation of attention has become the new frontier of human freedom." It is not the availability of choice that matters—it is *the architecture of incentives* that structures the choice field itself.

These architectures are rarely visible. They live in algorithmic ranking systems, interface hierarchies, and API design decisions. A platform like YouTube recommends videos based on watch history, but it also weighs watch time, click-through rates, content velocity, and advertiser preferences. A user looking for educational content may be funnelled toward entertainment that performs better in the algorithm. The platform did not prohibit learning—it simply *prioritised engagement*. Over time, this shapes what users come to expect, seek, and settle for. *The invisible hand of the incentive structure becomes the sculptor of desire.*

This is not limited to entertainment. Job boards, dating apps, fitness trackers, productivity tools—all are shaped by systems that embed assumptions about what success looks like. On LinkedIn, visibility is correlated with activity—likes, posts, endorsements. This rewards performative networking over quiet competence. On Tinder, success is gamified through swipe volume and response rates, not long-term compatibility. On Duolingo, language learning is structured through streaks and leaderboard points, which may enhance motivation but also shift focus from internal mastery to external validation. These shifts are not necessarily malicious. But they *are intentional*, and they inevitably shape how people define what it means to be good at something, or to be someone worth noticing.

What complicates the picture further is that most users *internalise these incentives without questioning them*. The psychological process is not one of coercion, but of alignment. The user wants to do well. The system tells them what "well" means. So they optimise their behaviour accordingly. A creator posts more often because the algorithm favours recency. A teenager deletes a photo that doesn't get enough likes. A professional updates their profile with performative language to rank higher in search. These are not acts of submission, but of *incentive conformity*. Over time, the platform's priorities become proxies for the user's own.

This is particularly consequential when platforms mediate fundamental human activities—communication, identity, decision-making. Facebook does not just host social interaction; it shapes *what kind* of interaction gets surfaced. Twitter (now X) does not merely publish thoughts; it amplifies those that perform best in metrics—often outrage or pith over nuance or care. The incentives favour a certain type of content, and thus a certain type of person: fast, reactive, brief, emotionally charged. Users learn to mirror this behaviour not because they are told to, but because *it works*. It gains reach. It garners response. The person they wish to be is slowly overwritten by the person the platform rewards.

Designers and technologists often argue that tools are neutral—that they reflect, rather than impose, values. But this stance evades responsibility. Tools may be neutral in their *potential*, but not in their *defaults*. Every design choice—what data is collected, what is surfaced, what is delayed—expresses a value judgment. Consider Google Search. A user assumes the top results are the most relevant. But relevance is calculated through hundreds of signals: freshness, authority, links, clicks, location, and more. That calculation has a logic, and that logic has consequences. If, for instance, commercial sites are favoured over nonprofit resources due to engagement metrics, the platform subtly shifts users' exposure to ideas without ever appearing to do so.

This asymmetry of understanding—between what platforms know and what users assume—is a defining feature of the modern internet. Users engage with what is presented, rarely questioning *why* it is presented. Few ask: What does this platform want from me? What behaviour is it incentivising? What values is it optimising for? In the absence of such questions, default settings become behavioural norms. As anthropologist Sherry Turkle observes, "We make our technologies, and then they shape us." The shaping is not overt. It is a quiet recalibration—away from reflection, toward reaction; away from self-determination, toward system alignment.

This does not mean users are helpless. Nor does it suggest that all incentives are corrupt. The problem is *opacity*. When systems optimise for hidden goals—be it attention, growth, data, or ad revenue—users are denied the ability to make informed choices. The interface hides the trade-offs. You see a notification, not a calculation. You experience frictionless convenience, not the economic imperative behind it. And because the system works—because it delivers dopamine hits, validates actions, facilitates connections—you are unlikely to question its deeper motives.

Ethical design requires reversing this opacity. It demands that platforms disclose their incentives, invite scrutiny, and align their success metrics with the well-being of their users—not just their engagement curves. Some attempts exist: Apple's Screen Time, Mozilla's privacy tools, DuckDuckGo's ad-free search model. These are small countercurrents in a sea of incentive structures optimised for extractive interaction. But they point toward a necessary reimagining: a digital ecosystem that treats users not as targets for behavioural manipulation, but as *agents with long-term goals of their own.*

To understand the full power of digital incentives, one must resist the myth that the user is sovereign. Control in digital systems is less about explicit commands and more about *framing*. You are free to choose—among options that have already been shaped. You are free to speak—but the algorithm determines who hears. You are free to seek truth—but relevance is defined by someone else's formula. The key question, then, is not "what can I do on this platform?" but *"what is this platform trying to get me to do?"*

Most people will not ask that question. Not because they lack intelligence, but because the interface discourages it. It wants to be used, not interrogated. But if autonomy is to mean anything in the digital age, it must begin with that question. Invisible intentions do not stay invisible forever. They show themselves in what we prioritise, how we spend our time, what we believe is worth doing. And unless we interrogate those structures, we may find ourselves optimising not for what we value—but for what the system values for us.

Addiction by Design

There is nothing accidental about how often people reach for their phones, open an app without thinking, or check notifications within seconds of waking. What feels spontaneous is, in fact, carefully choreographed. The digital tools that now shape daily life—social platforms, news feeds, video apps, productivity trackers—are not passive instruments awaiting instruction. They are environments engineered to provoke behaviour, sustain engagement, and encourage return. At the heart of this machinery is *persuasive technology*, the science of shaping human behaviour through design. And while its origins are rooted in the benign-sounding promise of "habit formation," its results often edge uncomfortably close to compulsion.

The term "persuasive technology" was popularised by BJ Fogg, a Stanford researcher who founded the Persuasive Technology Lab (now known as the Behaviour Design Lab). Fogg's framework, which became foundational to Silicon Valley's product culture, outlined how digital products could influence users' decisions by combining three elements: motivation, ability, and a trigger. If something is easy to do, aligned with a desire, and prompted at the right time, it becomes a habit. This principle was eagerly absorbed by platform designers, app developers, and growth hackers—not to support users' goals, but to *increase retention and engagement*.

Tristan Harris, a former Google ethicist and now co-founder of the Center for Humane Technology, has described the digital landscape as an arms race for attention. In Harris's view, platforms are not competing to make the best tools, but to create the most irresistible ones. Notifications are timed to reinforce reward loops. Content is auto-played to prevent reflection. Infinite scroll removes stopping cues. The result is a system that does not merely reflect user preference—it *steers* it. And it does so by targeting the same cognitive vulnerabilities exploited in casinos and slot machines.

Consider the principle of variable rewards. Unlike predictable feedback, intermittent rewards—rewards that come at unpredictable intervals—are far more effective at reinforcing behaviour. This insight, rooted in the work of psychologist B.F. Skinner, has become a design staple. When you refresh your email, scroll a feed, or pull to update, you are gambling: most of the time, you receive nothing noteworthy, but occasionally, something gratifying appears. That unpredictability keeps you hooked, because your brain anticipates the possibility of reward and releases dopamine in preparation. The reward becomes less important than *the anticipation of it*. You keep returning, not because the last experience was rewarding, but because the next one might be.

Nir Eyal's *Hooked: How to Build Habit-Forming Products* codified this into a template for digital success. Eyal's Hook Model consists of four phases: trigger, action, variable reward, and investment. The trigger initiates behaviour—say, a notification. The action is the user's response—opening the app. The variable reward delivers novelty, validation, or stimulation. And the investment—liking, posting, commenting—increases the likelihood of repeating the loop. Eyal maintains that such design can be ethical if aligned with users' true goals. But in practice, the line between helping users and exploiting them blurs quickly, especially when financial incentives reward time spent, not time well spent.

These systems are not neutral. They reflect commercial imperatives. The more a platform captures attention, the more data it gathers, the more ads it can serve, and the more revenue it generates. This attention-centric model incentivises the design of *digital environments that mimic addiction*, even if that word is rarely used in corporate meetings. As Harris has argued, the most powerful tech companies do not sell products—they sell *users' attention to advertisers*. The user becomes the resource being mined, not the customer being served.

What's particularly troubling is how these engineered environments shape not just habits, but identities. If a person spends three hours a day on TikTok, two on Instagram, and another hour checking email and messages, those are not just moments of attention—they are *slices of life*. They constitute the terrain on which moods form, relationships are maintained, values are reinforced, and self-perceptions evolve. To design for addiction is to participate in the shaping of human experience at a foundational level. It is not merely about screen time—it is about *who we become in the process of being captured*.

Importantly, not all engagement is unhealthy, and not all habit loops are manipulative. A meditation app may use notifications to encourage consistency. A fitness tracker may celebrate milestones to build motivation. These uses are not inherently exploitative. The key distinction lies in alignment. Is the design serving the user's long-term interests, or merely harvesting their short-term impulses? Is it helping them become who they want to be, or anchoring them in patterns they later regret?

This distinction is often obscured by metrics. Platforms optimise for quantifiable outcomes—time spent, sessions opened, clicks made. But *the quality of the experience* is rarely measured. Did the user feel better or worse after using the app? Did it help them focus, or fragment their attention? Did it enrich their relationships, or flatten them into metrics of approval? These are harder questions to answer, and harder still to monetise. So they are ignored. The system evolves not toward what is meaningful, but toward what is measurable.

The consequences of this evolution are becoming more visible. Digital wellbeing studies increasingly show correlations between excessive screen time and anxiety, sleep disruption, attention fragmentation, and social comparison. Young users, in particular, are vulnerable to environments that exploit their developmental need for validation and peer approval. But these effects are not limited to the young. Professionals routinely report diminished capacity for deep work, fragmented focus, and a creeping sense of fatigue—not from doing too much, but from *doing too much of what feels shallow and compulsive.*

To recognise that these effects are *designed*, not accidental, is to reclaim agency. It means seeing the app not as a benign conduit, but as a persuasive system with goals of its own. It means noticing the trigger before the loop begins. It means resisting the assumption that what is easiest is what is best. It means asking: Who benefits from this interaction? What is being extracted? What am I becoming through repetition?

That last question is the most urgent. For in a world increasingly mediated by persuasive technology, it is not just what we do that changes—it is what we notice, prioritise, and remember. Our attentional patterns shape our cognitive landscape. If we spend our lives reacting to optimised stimuli, we may lose the capacity to choose what matters, or to tolerate boredom, ambiguity, or slowness. We may become, as Harris warns, "pale shadows of our full potential," always responding, rarely reflecting.

Design is never neutral. It encodes assumptions, embeds values, and directs behaviour. When it is optimised for engagement at any cost, it becomes a form of behavioural engineering—subtle, effective, and difficult to resist. The tools may still look like apps and platforms. But what they really build are *loops of dependence.* And unless we learn to see the loop, we remain in it—not as users, but as subjects of design.

When Values Are Coded In

Few users pause to ask what values are embedded in the platforms they use. Fewer still imagine that their daily digital routines—scrolling, swiping, posting, reacting—are shaped by moral frameworks not their own. But every interface design, every ranking algorithm, and every feature rollout is underpinned by decisions that privilege some behaviours over others, amplify certain voices, and suppress others. The architecture of digital space is not neutral—it is a terrain structured by choices that reflect assumptions about the good life, the ideal user, and the acceptable boundary between freedom and control. The danger lies not in the fact that platforms encode values, but in how invisibly and unaccountably those values are imposed.

A platform like Facebook does not merely connect people—it decides *which* people are seen first, which posts get traction, which content gets frictionlessly shared, and which silently disappears. That decision-making is often presented as "algorithmic," a term that evokes technical objectivity. But algorithms do not float free from human influence. They are constructed by teams with goals, pressures, incentives, and biases. Those goals may include user engagement, ad revenue, retention, or regulatory compliance. Rarely do they explicitly consider human flourishing, democratic vitality, or the moral development of users. Yet those are precisely the dimensions they shape.

This is the crux of the matter: platforms do not merely organise information—they *prioritise* it. They decide what is surfaced at the top of your feed and what is buried. They determine whether time-sensitive posts appear in chronological order or by relevance, and how relevance is defined. They reward behaviours that generate reactions, and reactions that drive clicks. Each of these is a value-laden decision, whether acknowledged or not. An interface that highlights outrage over nuance, speed over depth, or spectacle over substance is not just more addictive—it *promotes a vision of what matters*. The user absorbs those priorities not through formal teaching, but through repeated exposure. The result is not argument but assimilation.

Take TikTok's "For You" page, widely acknowledged as one of the most effective content delivery mechanisms ever created. Its algorithm is famously opaque, but its effects are clear: it promotes content that performs well in early testing groups, often favouring aesthetics, novelty, and emotional punch over substance or integrity. It punishes complexity. A nuanced educational video may reach far fewer users than a polarising soundbite. This is not a technological flaw—it is a design logic that prioritises *attention capture*. The value it encodes is not truth, nor usefulness, but shareability. And that logic replicates across platforms, from Instagram's aesthetic curation to YouTube's recommendation engine to X's (formerly Twitter's) viral mechanics.

To understand this as a moral issue requires moving beyond technical vocabulary. When a platform elevates quick hits over sustained reflection, it is making a judgment about what kind of discourse is worth supporting. When it suppresses nudity but permits graphic violence, it is imposing a cultural norm. When it nudges users toward immediate reaction, it is shaping the rhythms of cognition. Every nudge, friction point, and design choice exerts pressure on human agency—not by force, but by structuring the path of least resistance. And as every behavioural economist knows, most people follow that path.

The moral landscape of design becomes even more consequential when it is *invisible*. Unlike laws, which are debated in parliaments, or norms, which are negotiated in public discourse, platform rules are often opaque. Shadowbanning, throttling, amplification—all happen behind the curtain of proprietary code. Users may sense that some content does better than others, but they cannot audit the mechanisms. This asymmetry is not just informational—it is *ethical*. It concentrates decision-making power in the hands of a few designers, engineers, and executives, who determine the boundaries of expression for billions. It removes contestability from the very systems that shape public life.

This is not an abstract problem. During election seasons, platform design can influence political outcomes. During pandemics, it can shape public health behaviours. In the lives of teenagers, it can define the contours of self-worth, belonging, and shame. When YouTube recommends conspiracy videos in succession, or when Instagram's filters promote a homogenised beauty ideal, those are not side effects—they are *features emerging from coded priorities*. And because they operate below the threshold of awareness, they are rarely questioned. We adapt to them reflexively, not reflectively.

It would be easier if platforms simply declared their values. But most prefer the posture of neutrality, insisting that they merely host content, facilitate connection, or reflect what users want. This is both misleading and convenient. It allows them to avoid accountability while reaping the benefits of influence. But no tool is truly neutral. A hammer used to build or destroy does not escape the intention of its wielder. And in the case of platforms, the wielder is the design team, the business model, and the institutional culture that sets the product roadmap.

Consider the seemingly minor decision to default autoplay on or off. When autoplay is enabled, users consume more video, stay longer, and are less likely to pause. This benefits platform metrics. But it also reduces friction between desire and action. It collapses intentionality. It reinforces passive consumption over active choice. The result is not just longer sessions—it is a habituated mode of being, one where agency erodes subtly over time.

Or take the gamification of productivity apps. Many now include streaks, badges, or performance dashboards. On the surface, these motivate users. But they also encode a particular view of what success looks like—measurable, continuous, optimised. This narrows the spectrum of meaningful activity to what can be tracked and rewarded. It marginalises ambiguity, rest, or non-quantifiable growth. These tools don't merely support your goals—they *reshape them.*

This is where values and code become indistinguishable. When a feature becomes popular, it is often adopted elsewhere. What began as an experiment in one app becomes a norm across the industry. Instagram borrowed Stories from Snapchat. YouTube adopted Shorts. LinkedIn introduced reactions. These replications are not neutral—they carry with them embedded assumptions about visibility, attention, and interaction. As they spread, so do their values.

To recognise this dynamic is not to indict all design. Rather, it is to call for a deeper ethical literacy among creators and users alike. Designers must be aware that every choice—what is made visible, what is made effortless, what is made optional—expresses a stance on human behaviour. Users must learn to see the values encoded in their tools, to ask not only what they can do, but *what they are being shaped to do*.

Digital literacy is no longer just about knowing how to use platforms. It is about understanding how they use you. And that means learning to decode their values—both explicit and hidden. Who gets visibility? What gets rewarded? Which voices are silenced by friction or filtered by opaque policies? These are questions of justice, dignity, and power—not just usability.

In a democratic society, invisible architectures of influence deserve scrutiny. When power is exercised through design rather than decree, it becomes harder to resist. That is why moral awareness must be built into the design process—not bolted on as an afterthought. It requires not just ethical review boards or diversity consultants, but a philosophical reckoning with what it means to shape human behaviour at scale. For in a world where billions engage daily with code-built environments, *design is destiny*. And values, whether we admit them or not, are already in the code.

The Myth of the Neutral Tool

A search bar feels impartial. A "like" button appears innocuous. A smartphone's calendar, a recommendation feed, even an email client—all give the impression of serving without steering. This is the myth of neutrality in technology: that tools simply extend human capacity without directing it, that platforms merely host rather than shape, and that interfaces are value-free channels through which our intentions pass untouched. But this belief is neither empirically grounded nor philosophically tenable. Every tool reflects a worldview, whether through what it makes easy, what it makes invisible, or what it makes impossible. Design is never passive; it encodes assumptions about human behaviour, priorities, norms, and ultimately, how life *should* be lived.

This fiction of neutrality serves many interests—corporate, cultural, and psychological. It comforts the user by relieving them of suspicion. It protects designers from scrutiny by treating their decisions as apolitical. And it feeds a broader narrative in which technology is simply "progress," unburdened by moral complexity. But neutrality is not the absence of bias; it is often the concealment of it. What a tool facilitates and what it discourages are both the result of choices—some explicit, many implicit. And those choices guide behaviour as surely as laws or customs do, often more subtly.

Consider the seemingly trivial swipe gesture. On dating apps like Tinder, swiping right signals interest, left signals rejection. This binary interaction replaces nuanced communication with a frictionless motion. It is efficient, yes—but it also embeds a philosophy of disposability. People become profiles; desire becomes instinct; relationships begin with a gesture better suited to clearing notifications than encountering a human being. The tool works as intended, but it changes what it means to intend. What we want is increasingly shaped by *what the tool makes wanting easy*.

The illusion of neutrality also rests on the idea that tools are value-agnostic until used. A hammer, after all, can build or destroy. But digital tools are not static objects waiting for a hand—they are dynamic systems with defaults, nudges, and predictive models. A GPS app doesn't just show the way; it *recommends* a route, based on metrics like speed, traffic, and fuel efficiency. Embedded in that recommendation is a value judgment: time is paramount, scenic quality is secondary, local discovery irrelevant. The user rarely questions it, because the tool obscures its assumptions under the veneer of objectivity.

Search engines are another case in point. Google's algorithm does not return the "best" results; it returns results optimised for engagement, relevance (as defined by its models), and advertising frameworks. The top result isn't an answer—it is a projection of what the system thinks you want based on data trails and user profiling. This is not neutral—it is predictive steering, driven by design logic that privileges what is clickable, recent, and monetisable over what is accurate, diverse, or challenging. Yet because this logic is hidden behind an unassuming input field, it rarely provokes examination.

The same is true in productivity software. Consider Microsoft Outlook or Google Calendar. These tools assume a model of work rooted in fragmentation and time-slicing. Meetings are slotted into thirty-minute blocks; focus is boxed into "available" time; the day becomes a grid. The interface doesn't *cause* distraction or burnout, but it *normalises* a conception of time in which availability equals productivity, responsiveness equals commitment, and busyness equals value. It codifies a worldview in which human attention is infinitely segmentable, and where efficiency takes precedence over presence.

Design choices also reveal their worldview through *exclusion*. What is not supported by a tool is often as revealing as what is. Twitter (now X) allowed likes and retweets for over a decade before introducing features to moderate tone or prompt users to read articles before sharing. The assumption? That amplification matters more than reflection. That reach trumps thoughtfulness. Instagram removed chronological feeds not because it lacked the ability to display them, but because the algorithmic feed better served engagement metrics. Every omission is a declaration of priorities. The absence of an option is an act of *ideological compression*.

One of the most underacknowledged forms of bias lies in data modelling. Machine learning systems are trained on datasets that reflect historical patterns—many of which include inequality, discrimination, or skewed representation. When predictive tools inherit those patterns, they don't just replicate bias—they *legitimise* it. Consider hiring algorithms that rank candidates, policing tools that predict crime hotspots, or financial models that assess creditworthiness. Each presents itself as neutral, mathematical, and data-driven. Yet each can silently encode the prejudices of its training data, reframed as technical output. The neutrality is illusory; the worldview is inherited.

This problem is amplified when the designers themselves disavow responsibility. The mantra "we just build the platform" is a convenient abdication of influence. But platforms are not just passive scaffolds. They are *selective affordance machines*. YouTube affords autoplay. Slack affords constant availability. Amazon affords one-click purchases. Each of these "affordances" reduces friction in one direction while increasing it elsewhere. That asymmetry matters. It makes some behaviours habitual, others awkward. Over time, those affordances become habits, and habits become norms. The tool becomes not just a mirror of society, but a mould.

Philosopher Langdon Winner argued decades ago that artefacts have politics—that is, they embody forms of power and authority within their design. A bridge built too low for buses excludes a demographic. A freeway cutting through a neighbourhood imposes a value on whose mobility counts. The same logic applies digitally. A content moderation system that favours majority norms can silence marginalised voices. A facial recognition system trained on lighter skin tones can misidentify minorities with higher error rates. These are not technical glitches—they are *epistemic biases* baked into design. And yet, because they are mediated through code, they often escape moral scrutiny.

Neutrality is also a rhetorical shield. When confronted with criticism, many tech companies resort to saying that "the tool can be used for good or ill." But this evades the deeper question: *what kind of behaviour does the tool encourage by default*? The default matters because it sets the behavioural baseline. Most users do not customise settings, read documentation, or scrutinise permissions. They use what is given. And what is given reflects a vision of what use should look like. That vision is not universal—it is a worldview rendered in interaction patterns.

Even aesthetics encode assumptions. The minimalist white space of Apple products projects calm and control, but also privileges individualism and polish. The gamified dashboards of fitness trackers promote quantification over intuition. The frictionless flow of Uber assumes that human relations can be streamlined to a button press, bypassing deliberation, context, or reciprocity. None of these are "just" design decisions. They are manifestations of cultural values, ideological leanings, and economic imperatives.

To challenge the myth of neutrality is not to demand ideological purity. It is to ask for *honest accountability*. If a tool is optimised for speed, say so. If it nudges toward consumption, own that. If it encodes a bias, make it visible.

What is dangerous is not that tools have embedded worldviews—but that they pretend not to. The pretence of neutrality creates a vacuum where influence operates without resistance, and where design becomes a form of soft coercion.

Technologists, policymakers, and users must develop a more mature vocabulary to interrogate these forces. This means treating interface design not as a matter of convenience but as a matter of ethics. It means including philosophers, educators, sociologists, and psychologists in conversations long dominated by engineers and venture capitalists. It means understanding that when we adopt a tool, we are not just gaining capabilities—we are also *adopting the premises baked into that tool.*

Ultimately, the tools we use shape the people we become. They shape our attention, our choices, our relationships, and our sense of self. To believe they are neutral is to surrender the power to ask: *whose vision am I enacting?* That is the real myth—one that this chapter seeks to undo, not with alarmism, but with clarity. Neutrality, in the world of technology, is not a fact. It is a story told to avoid harder questions. Let us start asking them.

Chapter 10
Reclaiming the Manual Mode

When every system around us is tuned for efficiency, the cost is not merely convenience—it is the subtle erosion of presence, attention, and authorship over our own lives. In a culture that prizes seamlessness, choosing to slow down, to act manually, to pause before proceeding, can feel both radical and restorative. This chapter opens not with a critique of technology, but with a deeper reckoning: the tools intended to enhance life often end up steering it, quietly usurping the scaffolding of autonomy—the capacity to determine not just what we do, but how we do it. This is not a nostalgic defence of the analogue, nor a blanket rejection of the digital; it is an invitation to regain orientation within systems designed to outpace thought.

The challenge lies not in the tools themselves, but in passivity. Defaults calcify into norms, swipes replace decisions, and habits are downloaded rather than learned. Every layer of abstraction—every algorithmic shortcut, every interface meant to "just work"—risks obscuring the processes it supplants. The result is fluency without comprehension, convenience without context. A GPS can deliver us flawlessly to a destination we would struggle to locate on a map. A camera applies filters whose mechanics elude us. A calendar nudges us into meetings we never paused to schedule with care. These tools are not flawed; their quiet success fosters dependence unnoticed. When life is lived entirely on autopilot, we become users of systems we no longer interrogate.

Reclaiming manual engagement is not a Luddite retreat; it is a strategic, selective reintroduction of friction. Friction, here, is not resistance for its own sake—it is a catalyst for reflection.

Writing by hand, for instance, imposes slowness that is not inefficiency but opportunity: space for thought to settle, memory to consolidate, cognition to deepen. In contrast, tapping notes into a phone is rapid, searchable, but often fleeting and unprocessed. Likewise, navigating by memory rather than following a blue dot activates spatial reasoning, cultivates orientation, and deepens one's sense of place. The former cultivates; the latter performs. Choosing friction here is a deliberate reassertion of agency, not an embrace of difficulty for its own sake.

The question is not whether to reject tools, but how to curate their influence. One need not abandon maps to practice navigation, nor forsake automation to maintain skill. The power lies in discernment: knowing when to offload and when to engage. In cognitive terms, this is not a question of rejecting comparative advantage, but recognising cognitive equity. Just because a tool can do something faster does not mean it should do so every time. Brewing coffee by hand, balancing a chequebook without an app, planning a week on paper—these acts slow us down, yes, but they also restore choice. And choice, exercised consciously, underpins agency.

A second consideration is the selective retirement of tools. Not every convenience justifies its presence. Our digital environment teems with options—apps for meditation, plugins for focus, interfaces for thought—but many add layers between us and the acts themselves. Meditation becomes another screen exercise; focus is toggled on or off. The challenge is not only to select tools, but to cull those whose presence has become reflexive rather than necessary. Functional honesty demands we ask: does this tool enhance clarity, or perpetuate dependency?

Constraint design offers insight here. Properly applied, constraints reveal rather than limit freedom. Artists have long known this: a sonnet's metre sharpens language, a limited palette sparks invention. Likewise, device-free hours, dumbphone experiments, or longhand drafts catalyse attentiveness and creativity. These constraints are self-authored, deliberately reintroducing reflection into the flow of digital drift. They carve spaces where skill, thought, and focus can re-emerge—not grand revolutions, but tactical adjustments.

Perhaps most crucial is re-examining why we engage with technology. Escapism, novelty, mood regulation—these impulses are not inherently wrong, but they are poor long-term motivators. Mindful engagement requires habits that are transparent, examined, and aligned with purpose. Each use must provoke the question: does this tool serve me, or distract me? Does it illuminate values, or obscure them? Not all interactions with technology are instrumental, but acknowledging their function strengthens intentionality.

Finally, consider the power of small, intentional acts of re-agency. Turning off notifications, leaving the phone elsewhere, deleting an app for a week, walking without headphones, writing a to-do list by hand—these micro-decisions restore authorship. They are not about productivity hacks, but about sovereignty. Over time, these small acts accumulate—not into dramatic transformation, but into quiet reorientation. Presence, not perfection; authorship, not abstinence.

This chapter sits at the pivot of the book's broader argument. Previous chapters have diagnosed drift—how technology fosters dependence, obscures its values, and invites passivity. Here, the emphasis shifts: not resistance through rejection, but agency through deliberate design. A life lived in manual mode is not nostalgia; it is attentiveness. Tools are used, not inhabited; choices are seen, not reflexively followed. Reclaiming manual mode does not reject modernity—it rebalances the relationship between self and system. It asks, with clarity: what do I wish to become while I use these tools? And what am I willing to reclaim to get there?

Reintroducing Friction on Purpose

Convenience, though often mistaken for progress, is rarely neutral. It smooths surfaces, shortens processes, eliminates pauses—and in doing so, reshapes the very texture of our experience. Every technological advance that removes effort also removes a layer of engagement. When software anticipates our words, GPS reroutes us seamlessly, and one-tap interfaces replace multi-step decisions, something more than time is being saved. *What is being lost is the space in which reflection, choice, and meaning arise.* In a world engineered for frictionless flow, we must ask: What is the cost of never slowing down? And what might we regain if we *deliberately* reintroduced difficulty—not as a hindrance, but as a design for awareness?

Friction, in its most generative form, is not the enemy of productivity; it is the guardian of intentionality. A paper planner requires us to write out our priorities, rather than drag and drop them. A handwritten journal demands time and physical engagement, often drawing out thoughts that a digital note app would flatten into bullets. Cooking a meal from scratch forces attention to process, to taste, to heat and timing—restoring a felt sense of agency lost in the automated click of a food delivery. These frictions are not accidental inefficiencies. They are *structures of attention*—devices for re-entry into the moment, into ourselves.

To understand why friction matters, it helps to distinguish between functional and cognitive effort. Functional effort is the labour it takes to complete a task—stirring, chopping, writing, mapping. Cognitive effort is the awareness that attends it—the space in which meaning is assigned, remembered, and internalised. When a device removes the former without giving us room to engage the latter, the activity is completed, but the experience is bypassed. Automated tools collapse functional effort but rarely compensate with depth.

This is how convenience becomes impoverishment: *we remember what we struggle with; we forget what we swipe past.*

Reintroducing friction is therefore not about punishing ourselves with nostalgia or inefficiency. It is about engineering spaces in which attention can return. The writer who drafts an outline on index cards before turning to their laptop is not rejecting digital tools—they are scaffolding their focus. The manager who limits team chats to fixed hours is not being regressive—they are protecting depth from ambient interruption. These acts of resistance are subtle, often private, and profoundly consequential. They do not aim to overthrow technology, but to reinstate sovereignty over *how* it is used.

Consider the emerging field of constraint design, which reframes limits as instruments of liberation. Within digital interfaces, this might mean greyscaling the phone screen to reduce allure, setting app timers not to enforce productivity but to make compulsion visible, or disabling autoplay to create an intentional break in consumption. Outside the screen, it might look like choosing to walk without headphones—letting silence accompany movement—or using cash for discretionary purchases to feel the weight of spending. These frictions do not inconvenience so much as *illuminate*. They return the locus of control to the user—not as a gesture of discipline, but as a restoration of choice.

To be clear, friction does not guarantee insight. A handwritten list can be as thoughtless as a voice command. A slow process can still be rushed in mind. But friction *enables* insight by creating the conditions in which awareness can surface. Without friction, everything moves too fast to reflect. There is no gap in which to ask: *Is this how I want to spend my time? Is this worth my attention? Is this serving the person I'm trying to become?* These are not abstract questions; they are the hinges upon which a mindful life turns. And they are rarely answered in the middle of speed.

One illuminating contrast is between analogue and digital task management. A to-do list app is efficient, scalable, and instantly editable—but also infinitely expandable and easily ignored. A paper planner, by contrast, imposes physical limits: space constraints force prioritisation, and the act of crossing something out carries more permanence than deleting. The friction of paper *sharpens discernment.* It makes visible the difference between what we *can* do and what we *should* do. In a digital tool, tasks multiply endlessly because there is no surface resistance. This is the paradox: in attempting to make life easier, digital tools can quietly make it *less livable.*

This principle applies just as clearly in communication. A handwritten letter slows the sender down and focuses the recipient. It requires effort, yes—but it also carries weight. Contrast this with the vanishing effort of instant messaging, where a reply is composed, sent, and forgotten in seconds. There is no time for revision, tone-checking, or emotional calibration. What is saved in speed is often lost in substance. By reintroducing friction—say, by pausing before responding, or composing difficult messages offline first—we don't just change how we communicate; *we change how we think* about what we're communicating.

It is easy to misunderstand friction as the opposite of flow. In fact, it is often the precondition for it. Mihaly Csikszentmihalyi's concept of "flow"—a state of deep immersion and satisfaction—arises not from ease but from challenge that matches ability. Friction, properly applied, is how we enter flow. It creates thresholds, commitment points, a sense of earned momentum. A runner warms up not just to avoid injury, but to cross into focus. A painter lays out their materials not to waste time, but to signal that *something matters.* Friction prepares the mind to arrive.

This insight has implications for how we design not only our tools, but our days. Morning rituals, device boundaries, closing rituals, analogue interludes—these are not productivity tricks.

They are *design decisions* about the rhythm of attention. Consider the difference between checking email first thing and starting the day by writing down three intentions. The first invites reactivity; the second *designs for authorship*. Both are small acts. But only one begins with pause.

Even in digital design, some creators are beginning to build friction back in. The meditation app Headspace inserts gentle animations before each session—not for branding, but to *slow the user down*. Email services like Hey require senders to be approved before reaching the inbox, imposing a friction layer to protect attention. Apps like Notion and Obsidian support slow, layered writing workflows rather than reactive publishing. These are design philosophies, not just features. They signal a shift from designing for habit-formation to designing for *awareness-formation*.

Of course, friction can become punitive. Not all effort is productive. If the barrier is too high, users disengage. If the constraint is artificial, it breeds frustration. The goal is not to burden every task with unnecessary ritual, but to *intentionally shape the cognitive environment* in which we operate. Like physical posture, attention has its ergonomics. A standing desk won't fix burnout, but it can change how we inhabit our work. Likewise, choosing friction won't make our days perfect—but it can render them more *inhabited*.

What this all points to is a deeper philosophical shift: from speed to presence, from automation to *participation*. In an attention economy that profits from passivity, choosing to reintroduce friction becomes a mode of self-authorship. It is not a return to a mythical past but an articulation of a different future—one in which the self is not a byproduct of design systems, but a co-author of them. When we design our environments to include effort, we do more than resist convenience. *We recover our capacity to notice, to care, and to choose.*

To live with deliberate friction is to reclaim time as more than throughput. It is to remind ourselves, again and again, that how we do something changes what that something becomes. That the act of boiling water for tea can be more than hydration—it can be pause. That handwriting a note can be more than messaging—it can be meaning. That walking without a device can be more than exercise—it can be *returning*. These are not metaphors. They are design strategies for a life not optimised to escape effort, but shaped to encounter it—with clarity, dignity, and presence.

Selective Forgetting of Tools

Not every tool we adopt deserves to stay in the toolbox. The march of convenience has outpaced our ability to discern which technologies genuinely serve us and which merely seduce. Modern life is saturated with applications, services, and platforms that promise speed, ease, and enhancement—but few ask whether that promise is worth fulfilling. The silent premise of most digital design is *more is better*—more automation, more delegation, more frictionless access. But an uncomfortable truth remains: *convenience can quietly displace competence, presence, and discernment.* Sometimes, the most powerful choice is to forget a tool, not because it fails, but because it succeeds too well at removing us from ourselves.

The idea of "tool abandonment" is almost heretical in a culture that treats every technological upgrade as an unqualified gain. But in systems thinking, forgetting is a form of adaptation. Ecologists speak of "adaptive forgetting"—a process by which organisms unlearn dependencies that no longer serve their changing environment. Similarly, in human behaviour, the conscious neglect of certain tools is not regression; it is *strategic calibration.* It allows us to align our technological environment with who we intend to become, rather than who the designers of our tools presume us to be.

To unlearn a tool, we must first identify which conveniences are *mutually valuable*—that is, which tools extend our capabilities without hollowing out our presence. Some tools are unambiguously helpful: spectacles, plumbing, fire. They extend human potential without supplanting fundamental capacities. Others, however, operate more ambiguously. A calendar app might help us manage our week—but if it makes scheduling so fluid that we abandon time-blocking, ritual, or focused periods of deep work, we have traded precision for pliability. A password manager that stores dozens of logins is efficient—until it severs any mental tether to our digital identity and erodes even basic memory. In these cases, the tool doesn't merely serve us—it *replaces* us in subtle ways.

A useful distinction emerges between *empowerment tools* and *replacement tools*. Empowerment tools extend human faculties—augmenting vision, amplifying voice, enhancing cognition. Replacement tools, by contrast, allow us to bypass those faculties altogether. The former promotes *engagement with the task*; the latter promotes *abandonment of the task*. A GPS app that teaches you to navigate better over time may be empowering; one that turns every journey into blind following is not. A budgeting tool that fosters awareness of spending patterns is useful; one that passively automates all financial decision-making may end up removing learning altogether. *Tools that do the work for you are not the same as tools that teach you how to work better.*

Some of the most culturally sticky tools—social feeds, autocorrect, voice assistants—are designed to feel indispensable. But their primary optimisation is for ease, not elevation. These are the tools most worth forgetting, at least periodically. Not because they are inherently harmful, but because their convenience masks *cognitive displacement*. They habituate us to outsourced decision-making, to the comfort of being nudged, reminded, auto-filled, or tagged. When used constantly, they risk decoupling action from awareness. The process becomes invisible, and with it, *so do we*.

To forget a tool is not necessarily to delete it. It may mean deliberately limiting its use, making it less accessible, or interrupting its default role in our routine. Consider someone who chooses to use maps only to locate their destination but not for turn-by-turn guidance. Or someone who types notes in a digital file but outlines them first by hand. These aren't affectations. They are *designs for cognition.* By altering the role a tool plays in a sequence, we reshape how knowledge is constructed and retained. This is not anti-technology—it is post-naïve technology: a mature, conscious relationship in which utility is not confused with virtue.

In many ways, this selective forgetting resembles the principles of minimalist design. In architecture, deliberate absence creates space for presence. A room that is too full does not accommodate the mind; it overwhelms it. In digital life, the same logic applies. A screen cluttered with apps does not expand opportunity—it fractures focus. The removal of a tool is often the *introduction of an experience.* Removing autoplay revives the pause. Removing email notifications restores depth. Removing instant messaging reintroduces *deliberateness* to communication.

There is also a moral dimension. Tools carry embedded assumptions—not just about what can be done, but about what *should* be done. A "Like" button assumes affirmation is valuable. A retweet function assumes amplification is neutral. A default setting assumes homogeneity of user needs. When we uncritically use tools, we silently consent to their embedded values. But when we evaluate—and sometimes forget—a tool, we interrogate those values. We reclaim moral agency over what we surface, what we suppress, and how we shape our interactions. *The tools we keep are expressions of what we believe should be easy, and what should remain effortful.*

Selective forgetting is also about psychological ecology. Every tool we interact with makes a claim on our cognitive environment. Some leave residue—open loops, ambient anxieties, notifications masquerading as needs. Others create mental dependency—on tracking, reminders, rankings. The more we forget to self-initiate, the more we wait to be told. This drift toward reactive living can be reversed only by subtractive discipline: curating which tools get to shape our attention, and which are shown the door.

It may be useful here to apply a diagnostic lens. Ask, of any tool you regularly use:

Does this tool extend or replace my cognitive effort?

When I don't use it, do I feel disoriented—or newly aware?

Has it made me more thoughtful over time, or just faster?

If I removed it for a week, would my values become clearer or more confused?

These are not efficiency questions; they are *alignment* questions. They bypass the trap of convenience metrics and get to the deeper matter of whether a tool serves who you want to be—not just what you want to do.

One real-world example is the growing popularity of "distraction-free writing tools"—apps like iA Writer, Ulysses, or OmmWriter. These are not functionally superior to Word or Google Docs. What they offer is *less*. Fewer buttons, fewer features, fewer paths out of thought. By limiting options, they increase intentionality. They exemplify the principle that sometimes, forgetting what a tool can do is what makes it useful. In a similar vein, analogue cameras are enjoying a revival—not because they outperform smartphones, but because they impose constraint. Every shot matters. Every frame costs something. *Slowness becomes a feature, not a flaw.*

It is tempting to think that maturity in technology use comes from mastering more tools. But often it comes from using fewer—more wisely. There is strength in being able to live without what you have. And there is clarity in knowing when to let go of what merely feels helpful. Selective forgetting is not about going backwards. It is about choosing tools that carry *the weight of their own necessity.*

To forget a tool on purpose is to remind ourselves of the difference between capability and wisdom. Capability is the ability to do something. Wisdom is knowing when not to. Most tools are designed to increase the former. Very few teach the latter. That part is up to us.

Designing for Awareness, Not Escape

It is not technology itself that diminishes human agency, but the way it is absorbed uncritically into daily life. What disempowers is not the device in one's hand, but the unconsciousness of the hand that reaches for it. Every time we swipe, click, scroll, or delegate, a tiny decision is made—yet most of these decisions occur beneath the threshold of awareness. We are not always escaping reality with technology; sometimes, more insidiously, we are escaping *awareness* of how we live. This distinction is crucial, and it sets the stage for a more mature response to the digital environment—not one of wholesale rejection, but one of active redesign.

The dominant cultural response to technological overwhelm tends to oscillate between addiction and abstinence. On one end are users drowning in hyper-connectedness, on the other, calls for digital detoxes, unplugging weekends, or minimalist retreats. But neither extreme engages the real challenge: *how to inhabit technology without being subsumed by it.* The goal is not to escape the tools but to see through them—to cultivate a lens that renders design visible, habits legible, and motivations transparent. This is not digital asceticism. It is the pursuit of *tech-literacy as personal sovereignty.*

To design for awareness means engineering friction back into our engagements—*not to obstruct function but to restore reflection.* The default setting of modern design is to eliminate delay, smooth over decision points, and predict preferences. Platforms learn what we want and serve it before we articulate it. That is remarkable. But it is also a subtle erosion of the muscle of *choice awareness.* In many cases, the speed and seamlessness of digital experiences displace the cognitive pause in which intention forms. The question becomes: what small redesigns—of tools, habits, workflows—can make intention more probable than impulse?

Start with the device itself. Consider the home screen of a smartphone. For most users, it is optimised for frequency, not value: the apps we use most—messaging, news, social media—tend to be the most prominent. But what if the screen were redesigned for aspiration instead of routine? What if apps that reflect personal priorities—language learning, mindfulness, journaling—were surfaced first, and dopamine-chasing distractions tucked away? A change in layout is a change in narrative: from *what pulls me most* to *what matters most.* This is not just UI management—it is behavioural architecture with ethical weight.

Some product designers already understand this principle. The concept of "calm technology," coined by Mark Weiser and John Seely Brown in the 1990s, proposed that technology should inform but not demand attention. The most human-centred designs, they argued, are those that recede into the periphery unless truly needed. Yet the commercial internet has largely evolved in the opposite direction—toward apps that *compete* for attention rather than *coordinate* with intention. The challenge, then, is not simply what the tech can do, but *how we design our relationship to it.*

That relationship begins with habits. Habit formation is not just a behavioural concern; it is a political act. To adopt a new routine is to vote for a certain self, to declare allegiance to certain values. Yet most digital habits form passively, shaped by external incentives rather than internal convictions. The notification badge, the infinite scroll, the autoplay feature—these are not neutral design decisions. They are expressions of a platform's priorities. And unless countered by *deliberate counter-design*, they easily become habits of the hand, and eventually, habits of the mind.

Designing for awareness means refusing default settings when they don't serve you. It means reclaiming agency not through rejection, but through reconfiguration. For example, turning off push notifications is not about ignoring the world. It is about reestablishing boundaries for how and when the world enters your attention. Choosing a paper calendar over an app may seem quaint, but it reintroduces the tactile memory and spatial awareness that digital scheduling often strips away. Even something as simple as using a dedicated alarm clock instead of a phone can alter the first and last 15 minutes of a day—those vulnerable, formative moments where attention is most malleable.

Yet awareness is not simply about resisting tech's influence. It's also about *understanding its grammar.* Just as literacy in language enables one to read critically rather than passively, tech-literacy enables one to *discern affordances, incentives, and asymmetries.* Most users cannot describe how algorithmic feeds operate, how privacy settings are structured, or how content curation decisions are made. That ignorance is not neutral—it tilts the power dynamic in favour of the platform. As digital citizens, *understanding the logic of the systems we inhabit is as foundational as understanding the laws of the state.* Awareness, then, is a civic competence.

This is why personal sovereignty in the digital age begins not with escape, but with literacy. Not just technical literacy, but ethical, attentional, and behavioural literacy. What does this app want from me? What am I trading for convenience here? Who benefits from my frictionless interaction? These are not paranoid questions. They are structural ones. They expose the real transaction beneath the glossy UI. Most platforms are built not to empower users but to convert engagement into revenue. Knowing that changes how we participate. *Designing for awareness is designing for discernment.*

Importantly, this is not a call for constant vigilance. Hyper-awareness is exhausting and unsustainable. The aim is *strategic awareness*—knowing where to intervene, what to monitor, and where to trust. It's about establishing enough meta-cognition to notice when you've drifted from intention, and enough system fluency to adjust course. Consider the analogy of driving: you don't consciously monitor every muscle involved, but you do maintain situational awareness—of speed, terrain, traffic, direction. The same is true for tech engagement. Most of it can run in the background, as long as some key signals remain foregrounded.

There are promising design responses emerging from this ethos. The "digital well-being" tools on smartphones that show screen time trends, app limits, and focus modes are a step in this direction—not because they force behaviour, but because they *surface patterns.* Similarly, browser extensions that replace algorithmic feeds with mindful prompts, or minimalist operating systems that restrict multitasking, are not escapes from technology—they are escapes *into* better awareness. These tools do not assume users are weak; they assume users are *human.*

Mindful redesign also extends to culture. Families, workplaces, and schools each encode their own digital norms—some conscious, most inherited. A workplace where "respond instantly" is the unspoken rule creates a rhythm of urgency that rewires attention. A family where phones are always present at meals embeds availability as a norm.

Cultural redesign means creating *collective frictions*—tech-free meetings, phone-free dinners, email blackout hours—not to punish, but to *protect what needs protecting.* Awareness is not only personal; it is environmental.

And yet, the deeper point is psychological. Escape is a reactive move. It implies loss of control. Awareness, by contrast, is proactive. It creates space between stimulus and response. Viktor Frankl famously said that "between stimulus and response, there is a space. In that space is our power to choose our response. In our response lies our growth and our freedom." Applied to technology, *designing for awareness is the act of enlarging that space.* Not to retreat from the digital world, but to enter it with eyes open, values intact, and sovereignty preserved.

To live well with technology is not to shun it, but to *stay awake* within it. The tools will continue to evolve, the interfaces will become more seamless, and the incentives will always lean toward more: more engagement, more integration, more automation. But awareness is the one variable that can't be engineered on your behalf. It must be chosen, designed for, and cultivated. And the cost of neglecting it is not merely distraction—it is the quiet surrender of the self to systems we do not fully understand.

This is not a message of alarmism. It is a call to design differently—not for escape, but for clarity. Not to return to the past, but to navigate the future with *mindful presence*. The most important technology is not the one in your pocket. It's the *architecture of your attention*. And that, more than any algorithm, is yours to shape.

Small, Intentional Acts of Re-Agency

There is a quiet revolution available to anyone with a smartphone in their pocket: the choice to act *deliberately* in a system designed for automaticity. In an age where so much of digital life unfolds in the absence of conscious choice—feeds that refresh themselves, notifications that beg for attention, settings that configure themselves—reclaiming even a sliver of volition can be a radical gesture. Agency, in this context, does not require grand declarations or wholesale rejections of technology. It begins with *small, intentional acts*—simple adjustments that signal you are present, alert, and participating on your own terms.

Re-agency is not about wrestling control away from machines, but about *restoring authorship* to the rhythms of your life. This distinction is essential. Autopilot is not evil—it is efficient. Cognitive offloading allows us to focus on higher-order thinking. But there is a cost when too many behavioural routines become ambiently governed by default design, especially when those defaults align more with platform goals than personal ones. The alternative is not constant scrutiny or tech-paranoia. It is *low-friction counter-design*—nudges, rituals, and models that gently reinsert self-awareness into the loop.

Consider, for example, the act of checking your phone. Most people do it dozens, even hundreds of times per day, often without realising it. The behaviour is rarely preceded by a conscious decision—it is triggered by a moment of boredom, a ping, a fleeting thought. But what happens if that behaviour is interrupted, not with discipline, but with design? A simple prompt—like a lock screen that asks "What are you looking for?"—can restore a sliver of cognitive friction. That question doesn't shame or block; it invites pause. It reminds the user that behind every habit lies a hypothesis about need.

These micro-interventions matter because they scale. A single act of pausing before clicking can, over time, reshape patterns of engagement. BJ Fogg, a behavioural scientist at Stanford, has long argued that behaviour change happens not through willpower but *environmental scaffolding*. His model—Behaviour = Motivation + Ability + Prompt—reveals that if you want to change the outcome, you can either increase motivation (hard), increase ability (slightly easier), or adjust the prompt (simpler still). In digital life, the prompt is often invisible. By making it visible—or by reengineering it entirely—we shift the terrain of action.

One practical application of this is the "displacement principle." If a digital habit is unwanted—say, checking social media too frequently—the goal is not to remove the trigger but to *replace the behaviour it initiates*. For instance, moving the app off the home screen does not eliminate its existence, but it adds just enough friction to invite reconsideration. More powerfully, one can replace it with a healthier default: placing a journaling app, meditation icon, or reading shortcut in its place. The phone remains, but its grammar changes. The story it tells about your time becomes more aligned with your values.

Another behavioural frame with wide utility is the *Implementation Intention*, a concept pioneered by psychologist Peter Gollwitzer. Unlike vague goals ("I should check email less"), implementation intentions are specific, situational commitments: "If I feel the urge to open Instagram during work hours, I will instead write down one thing I'm avoiding." This small structural shift—linking a cue with a concrete alternative—dramatically increases follow-through. It creates a plan the mind can access in real time, reducing the cognitive load required to override habit.

These aren't productivity hacks. They are tools of *self-definition*. The goal is not optimisation for its own sake, but recovery of authorship. The prevailing logic of digital life is "more"—more speed, more efficiency, more connection. But agency is often found in *less*: fewer default responses, fewer compulsive loops, fewer assumptions about what technology must be. Re-agency means interrogating not just the tools you use, but *why* you use them, and *who you become* in the process.

This is where mental models become indispensable. One of the most powerful is the "Choice Architecture" concept from behavioural economics. First introduced by Richard Thaler and Cass Sunstein, it refers to the way environments can be structured to influence decision-making. Most people assume that tech choices are made freely, but the architecture of those choices—layout, defaults, framing—exerts tremendous power. To reassert agency, one must first see the scaffolding. Then, wherever possible, reconstruct it.

That might mean changing notification settings to "off by default," or turning off autoplay features so that attention doesn't flow passively into the next stimulus. It could involve setting "focus modes" with tightly curated app access during different times of the day—essentially building personalised environments for thought, work, or rest. More subtly, it might mean keeping a physical notepad near your device to externalise intention before engagement: "Why am I reaching for this?" *The mere act of writing it down interrupts the loop, and makes the next action conscious rather than reactive.*

Another useful frame is *temporal bundling*, the idea that decisions are rarely isolated but accumulate over time into patterns of behaviour. It's not that opening your inbox at 9 p.m. is inherently bad—it's that doing it consistently creates a narrative where availability eclipses rest. Similarly, choosing a fast-paced podcast during a walk is not necessarily worse than walking in silence—but it slowly trains the mind to associate solitude with consumption rather than contemplation. Awareness of temporal bundling helps individuals ask: *What patterns am I reinforcing? What identity do these habits build over time?*

That brings us to perhaps the most powerful re-agency tool of all: reflection. The most effective interventions are not always real-time nudges, but retrospective audits. A simple weekly review—What tools did I use most? Which interactions left me energised or depleted? Where did I act by default, and where by design?—can surface trends invisible in the moment. Over time, these reflections become feedback loops. They reveal the delta between *how you lived* and *how you want to live.* And from that delta, new experiments emerge.

These experiments don't have to be dramatic. In fact, smallness is their strength. Try a "tech Sabbath" for half a day, not the full 24 hours. Use a feature phone one weekend per month. Move one core task—like calendar management—off your device and onto paper. Install a browser blocker not to restrict, but to prompt reflection. These actions don't need to become permanent. What matters is their *signal value*: they remind you that *you are capable of changing the rules.*

And perhaps that is the most underappreciated point. Digital life often gives the illusion of flexibility while reinforcing rigid defaults. Platforms adapt to preferences, yes—but only within pre-encoded constraints. True flexibility arises when the user becomes the *author of their own context.* Re-agency is not about resisting tools, but about *designing your own use-cases,* on your own terms. It is about recovering the *imaginative space* that allows you to ask, "What if I did this differently?"

The final insight is this: you don't need perfect consistency. You need *regular evidence* that agency is still available to you. That evidence can come from a pause before a click, a question before an app opens, a journal note before you check the news. These are not trivial acts. They are signals that your attention is not entirely colonised, that your habits can be renegotiated, and that your identity is still in play. In a world designed for drift, *even a small anchor counts.*

Agency doesn't begin with willpower. It begins with *awareness, followed by experimentation, followed by reflection.* That loop, repeated with care, becomes the foundation for a more intentional digital life—one that does not reject the modern world, but meets it with clarity, sovereignty, and a commitment to live as though your attention still belongs to you. Because it does.

About the Author

Rowan Hale writes at the intersection of technology, ethics, and human systems. With a background in behavioral analysis and urban systems, Hale explores how emerging technologies quietly reshape the architecture of daily life—often without our consent or awareness. Known for dissecting complex innovations with clarity and curiosity, Hale brings a deep interest in the unseen trade-offs behind convenience, automation, and digital infrastructure. Invisible Upgrades continues Hale's mission to help readers see the world not just as it is, but as it is being subtly redesigned.

www.ingramcontent.com/pod-product-compliance
Lightning Source LLC
Chambersburg PA
CBHW031343230926
51848CB00002B/369